PRAISE FOR **FEAR IS** *My Homeboy*

"Fear can be your best friend, and this book will be too! Judi's advice is relevant, relatable, and—most importantly—actionable!"

–MEL ROBBINS, Author of the International Bestseller, *The 5 Second Rule*

"This book is fantastic. It's your best girlfriend in a pink cover. It's your life coach and your funny sister and your favorite teacher all wrapped into one. Judi Holler is a woman you need in your life."

–VANESSA VAN EDWARDS, Author of *Captivate: The Science of Succeeding with People*

"*Fear Is My Homeboy* is a roadmap for anyone who has let fear, self-doubt, or insecurity stand in the way of designing a life they dream about. If you know you're meant for more, but not quite sure how to get out of your own way, do yourself a favor and pick up this book and let Judi light the path."

–CARA ALWILL LEYBA, Best-Selling Author and Master Life Coach

"If you've ever second-guessed yourself, experienced imposter syndrome, or been frozen in the moment (and let's face it, who hasn't?), this book is for you."

–JOSH MILES, Host of Obsessed with Design, Author of *Bold Brand 2.0*

"As the majority of regrets in life revolve completely around fear, Judi has made a tremendous impact using the ideas in this book to teach our sales teams on how to push through their fear so they can perform at a higher level. *Fear Is My Homeboy* is not just a title of her book, but the code on how she lives her life and inspires others. This book can such an important part of each person's personal journey!"

–MICHAEL DOMINGUEZ, Chief Sales Officer, MGM Resorts International

HOW TO **SLAY** DOUBT, **BOSS** UP,

AND **SUCCEED** ON YOUR OWN TERMS

FEAR IS My Homeboy

JUDI HOLLER

GREENLEAF
BOOK GROUP PRESS

Published by Greenleaf Book Group Press
Austin, Texas
www.gbgpress.com

Distributed by Greenleaf Book Group

For ordering information or special discounts for bulk purchases, please contact Greenleaf Book Group at PO Box 91869, Austin, TX 78709, 512.891.6100.

Design and composition by Greenleaf Book Group
Cover design by Greenleaf Book Group
Cover texture image copyright idiz, 2018. Used under license from Shutterstock.com
Social media icons made by Pixel perfect from www.flaticon.com

Publisher's Cataloging-in-Publication data is available.

Print ISBN: 978-1-62634-626-0

eBook ISBN: 978-1-62634-625-3

Part of the Tree Neutral® program, which offsets the number of trees consumed in the production and printing of this book by taking proactive steps, such as planting trees in direct proportion to the number of trees used: www.treeneutral.com

Printed in the United States of America on acid-free paper

20 21 22 23 24 25   14 13 12 11 10 9 8 7 6 5

First Edition

More by Judi Holler:

The #FearBoss Project Workbook

The Vibe and Thrive Planner

Learn more and join our brave community here!

You can't be brave unless you are scared first.

So, fear, this one's for you.

Contents

Preface

'm so glad you picked up this book. As a bookworm myself, some of my greatest heroes and mentors have been the authors who have had the guts to sit down and do the work, penning their own books to share their ideas with the world. These books have certainly changed my life, and I attribute reading books to most of my success because I truly believe books are the gateway to greatness!

I came up with the idea for Fear Is My Homeboy® when reading one of these brave books while on my honeymoon in January 2016. The book was *Big Magic* by Elizabeth Gilbert. Back then, I was already speaking and writing about improv theater, fear, and personal branding as my "side hustle," yet I was having trouble connecting all the dots. I was also stalling on quitting my job in destination sales and marketing so I could speak and write full-time. I was—gulp—scared to death. I had so many what-ifs running through my head and felt incredibly stuck. *Will I be able to pay my bills? Am I cut out for running a business? How do I run a business? Will anyone hire me? Who am I to be a keynote speaker? How does a website work?* Ah, the self-doubt.

So there I was, sitting in a tropical paradise with my new hubby, when my eyes landed on page 22 of *Big Magic*. The chapter was titled "The Fear You Need and the Fear You Don't Need." After reading the first few sentences, I got butterflies of excitement and quickly penned in the margin with a hot-pink highlighter: *Fear is my homeboy!* The "homeboy" part proudly declared fear as my friend; yet, if that was really the case, then why was I wasting so much time trying to get rid of it?

I knew deep in the core of my bones that I had figured something out. I knew I had uncovered the real secret in getting to the other side of fear, and I had to share it with the world.

When I got home, I rewrote my personal branding keynote and reframed its core message. I started focusing on the role of fear in our lack of opportunities and personal fulfillment. I came to realize that the only thing that holds us back from what we really want is fear, and this includes all of our excuses. Once I realized that excuses are one of the ways fear keeps us stuck, safe, and just the same, I took my power back and started having a different conversation with my fear.

Instead of wasting so much energy trying to get rid of my fear or outrun it, I realized it was time to take a deep breath and make space for it. For me, this means that when fear shows up, instead of letting it boss me around and call all the shots in my life, I needed to pause—to feel it, say hello, welcome it, and take a good look at it—because most of the time when fear shows up, it's there for a reason. Often it's there to show you what you need to do next.

I quit my job three months later. This was the first time I officially made fear my homeboy, and I've never looked back.

If Elizabeth Gilbert hadn't written page 22 of that book, I may not have written this book on fear. I shudder to think about that close call. It's also hard to think about how many incredible ideas are living inside people all over the world—and how so many of these people are afraid to let these ideas out. I'm on a mission to stop that from happening. I'm on a mission to stop fear from stealing your opportunities so you can slay doubt and succeed the way *you* want to succeed.

I am definitely not your guru. I'm just like you—I get scared and mess up. Sometimes I accidentally hurt people and get it wrong. But I accept all of these hard parts of my life, because they are a part of being human. My fear journey has given me the stories, ideas, and training to fill the pages of this book.

Because of my background as a professionally trained improviser and alumna of the Second City Training Center Conservatory in Chicago (a prolific improv comedy theater that is consistently a starting point for famous comedians and award-winning actors and directors), improv inspires all my work. Improv was also my most important fear training. I built a successful career in the hospitality and meetings industry while studying improv at night, so I know how to bridge the gap between the off-the-cuff comedy of improv and the seriousness of work. The ideas I share on fear will help you level up personally and professionally, and encourage you to make boss moves at work and in your industry. There will be lots of tips, tools, and practical takeaways that you can start using to make big shifts in your life. The only requirement is forward momentum!

I wrote this book on planes, in hotel rooms, at the library, in my office with my dog at my feet—most days in my jammies. I wrote this book from scribbles of thoughts I wrote on pages of books, from collections of ideas stored in my computer, and from all my line-filled notebooks while studying improv at the Second City Training Center Conservatory in Chicago. Most days I had no idea where to start. Most days I'd find myself procrastinating instead of doing the work because I was afraid of not being good enough. Most days I just stared at the blank screen, literally frozen with self-doubt. Then I saw fear sitting there with me, wanting me to stop and self-doubt and procrastinate so I wouldn't write this book. So, I took a deep breath, thanked my fear for reminding me I'm alive (feeling fear means you are still breathing!), and started writing. One word at a time, one day at a time. Forward momentum was my medicine.

If I can be here writing a book while terrified out of my mind, then I know you can do whatever your scary thing is too. Whatever you're facing, you are braver than you can even imagine.

So let's throw a party for you and your fear, so you can stop wasting time and start succeeding on your own terms. I can't wait to show you how.

Let's get this party started.

Fearfully *yet* courageously yours,

Introduction

"She was powerful not because she wasn't scared
but because she went on so strongly despite the fear."
—ATTICUS

'd like to start a fear movement with you, one where we redefine what it means to be afraid and flip the script on how fear shows up in our lives. The world is telling us to be fearless, yet their definition of "fearless" is not realistic; if you were truly fearless, you would put yourself into really dangerous situations and could end up physically hurt, or worse. You'd walk out into traffic, or walk alone down an alley at night, or never go to a doctor. If you were truly fearless, you'd end up in more dangerous situations than you'd ever want to encounter. Fear shows up to keep you in one piece.

Fear is your friend, your best friend, your business partner, and your homeboy. Why would we want to get rid of something that can keep us safe, be an incredible compass in our lives, shake us, wake us, and remind us that we are very much alive?

In order to see fear as your best friend, however, you will have to rethink how you think about fear. You will stop chasing being fearless and start welcoming fear to your life party by making space for your fear—tons and tons of space. This mindset shift will allow you to fear-LESS and start living more fear-FULLY. You'll realize that you will never be able to outrun, or get rid of, your fear, but you can befriend it—you can get really good at doing things even while feeling afraid. Making Fear Your Homeboy is this idea that when you aren't afraid to welcome fear into your house and are grateful for it, you can stand up to it when you need to and move forward courageously.

Making Fear Your Homeboy may look like being terribly nervous before a presentation but instead of trying to pretend that you aren't, you thank your fear because the nerves remind you that you have a heart beating in your chest. Making Fear Your Homeboy may look like someone studying for an exam and being filled with self-doubt, then doing what fear doesn't expect by reminding themselves how much they love themselves and how smart they are, rather than dreading the exam. Making Fear Your Homeboy looks like confronting a toxic person in your life while being grateful for the gift of the healthy relationships you do have to show you the difference.

Making Fear Your Homeboy means that you develop gratitude for your fear—and it's not easy. While it may feel a little uncomfortable at first, this notion of being grateful for feeling afraid will help you get stronger. You will stop wasting your precious energy trying to get rid of something you'll never be able to outrun in the first place.

It's Never Too Late

If you are reading this right now and think that you've missed your chance, that it's too late, that it's all been done before, that you've run out of time, that you're too old, too busy, not smart enough, not talented enough, not ready enough: you are wrong. In fact, you are probably suffering from the fear disease I like to call: SLAY-o-phobia.

> **SLAY-o-phobia:** (noun) A fear of success that causes a person to doubt their greatness and play it safe. Results in missed opportunities and a mediocre life.

The only cure for SLAY-o-phobia is making a choice to be brave. And you can't be brave unless you are scared first. You need your fear; it's how you become brave in the first place.

What Is Brave?

To be brave doesn't mean you have found a way to get rid of or conquer your fear. Being "brave" does not mean being fearless; however, being brave does mean that you fear-LESS. Braveness requires action. You can't sit there doing nothing and consider it being brave. Bravery is an organic process that comes from within, and it will look different for everyone.

You will have generational fears, which are those fears that show up and require you to be brave at different stages of your life. What you fear as a twenty-year-old is a lot different from the things you fear as a forty-year-old. Then you will have gendered fears, because men and women fear different things and process their fears differently. Regardless of your age or your gender, however, the common bravery denominator is action.

Bravery is doing something when you are afraid. It means doing the scary thing even though fear keeps whispering lies in your ear trying to stop you. Bravery knows better than to wait for the right time, because there never will be a right time. The time is *now*; otherwise, every day you are missing critical opportunities to connect in powerful and profitable ways simply because you lack the courage, and confidence, to do so.

> You self-doubt.
>
> You overthink.
>
> You procrastinate.
>
> You obsess.
>
> You wait.
>
> You worry.
>
> You stress.
>
> You stop.

Think of how many amazing gifts the world may be missing out on because you don't have the courage to shine bright like the diamond that you are.

Just imagine if . . .

Beyoncé never got into formation?

MJ never moonwalked?

Snoop Dogg never introduced himself to Dr. Dre?

The Rolling Stones felt there were too many rock bands?

Rosa Parks never stayed on that bus?

Neil Armstrong played it safe and thought becoming an astronaut was crazy?

Steve Jobs became a chef?

Just imagine the world without the invention of computers, cell phones, the internet, restaurants, food, airplanes, automobiles, hotels, and champagne. All of the things we love in this world required someone to be brave, to feel their fear and do it anyway. To trust themselves. To be crazy enough to think, *Why not me?*

We need what you have. We need you to show up. We need you to go scared.

We need what you have. We need you to show up. We need you to go scared.

How to Use This Book Like a Boss

I'd like to officially welcome you to the fear party. Our guest of honor is fear. At this party you will meet all kinds of characters, get to listen to tons of stories, and you'll probably get wasted on inspiration. But the best part? You'll wake up the next day with zero hangover, ready to boss up on your life. The only requirement at this fear party is being brave enough to have an open mind.

I'm going to tell some stories, teach some lessons, and share the ideas that have changed my life. Many of the doubt-slaying ideas in this book are inspired by what I've learned in improv theater, so you'll learn a lot of improv wisdom. This book is best read from front to back, as each chapter builds on the others and provides ideas and stories that tee up the next chapter's ideas and stories.

Here's what you can expect:

In chapter 1, we will talk about loving yourself. You can't make fear your homeboy and hate yourself; it's not possible. Loving yourself is mandatory because nothing else in this book will work for you if you can't. You will learn how to stop making excuses and start trusting the process.

In chapter 2, we'll get a little woo-woo and talk about the universe. This chapter is about trust, knowing that what's meant for you will come to you. Most importantly, we'll talk about how trusting yourself is just as important. You learn how to love your failures, catch more boomerangs, and find out what hustle really means.

In chapter 3, we invite balance to the party and talk about my favorite subjects: focus and productivity. We must understand how to balance our life because when we don't, it's easy for fear to slip in and make a mess of things. This chapter is all about how to regulate your schedule and stop letting your email boss you around.

In chapter 4, we will talk about bossing up—which means that you step up your game and take responsibility for the direction of your life—and how you can run the business of who you are like the CEO you were born to be. This chapter goes deep and covers many tactical ideas you can use both personally and professionally. You will learn how to assess trade-offs, become more google-licious, and toot your own horn without blowing it.

In chapter 5, we talk about the importance of building and loving your network so you don't have to manage your fear alone. Having a solid squad in your corner is a killer doubt-slaying tool. In this chapter, you'll learn who should (and should not) be invited to your life party, how to nurture your network, and that fear has a squad of its own.

In chapter 6, we welcome the magic of momentum to our fear party and discuss the power of staying in forward momentum. You will learn how to say yes, when to say no, and why "longcuts" (as opposed to shortcuts) matter.

In chapter 7, we land the plane and make sure the jet bridge is in place so you can go forth as the fear boss you now have become. You will learn how to celebrate your bravery, be the hero of your own story, and follow your bliss.

As you read this book, you'll notice that at the end of each chapter there are "homework" assignments. Each fear boss assignment was created to help you build upon the work presented in this book and incorporate the ideas into your life. You will be able to use these assignments both personally and professionally. You could most certainly use the homework as ideas or topics for your next team meeting at work. You could share the ideas in your book club to start fear conversations among friends and/or colleagues. Maybe you create a "fear boss reading circle" of your own where you discuss this and other bravery-inciting books in a group setting.

Last, I hope you read this book with a highlighter and your favorite writing instrument handy and make notes as you go. I hope this book is marked up, flagged, photographed, and Instagrammed—and one you call on again. Make sure you let me know what you love by using #FearIsMyHomeboy on all the social media sites so I can follow along in your journey.

Mostly, I hope you have as much fun reading this book as I did writing it.

Onward we go.

Cue the confetti.

CHAPTER 1

Love Yo'self

"She remembered who she was and the game changed."
—LALAH DELIA

Why do we wait for the bottom to drop out before we decide to take care of ourselves? Why do we wait for the diagnosis, the failed marriage, the lost job, the accident, the destroyed friendship, or the illness to wake up to what's really going on in our lives?

Guilt, self-doubt, and fear make you stick to your same ol' patterns because it's just easier that way. How could you possibly put yourself first when there are so many people that need you and depend on you? You are slammed, and stressed out, and running on all cylinders. You are taking care of kids, family, and/or a partner, plus trying to keep it together at work so you can earn that paycheck—all while trying to keep it together at home with a full fridge, clean toilets, and food on the table in time for dinner. By the time all that is done, who ends up last on your list? You. We're constantly putting ourselves last, every single time.

If you can't figure out how to love yourself first, you will never be able to make fear your homeboy. It's the #1 requirement; because if you don't love yourself, how can you expect anyone else to? When you love yourself more than anything, fear doesn't stand a chance because no matter what happens—good, bad, or ugly—you know you will be okay. Fear can't stand that. It hates when you love yourself because when you do, *you* become the boss, not fear.

Nothing Works Unless You Do

This idea is so damn juicy and important I should write it again:

Nothing works unless you do!

Yes, that is written in I'm-hollering-at-you-girl font on purpose. Why? Because sometimes we need to hear something loud and clear, multiple times, so it really sinks in. You are not a machine; you are a human being. If you aren't working, nothing else will. If you are miserable personally, it's going to affect you professionally. And if you are miserable professionally, it's going to affect you at home. The only constant in both scenarios is you.

This means that you have an incredible opportunity in front of you to flip the script. See, when you love and take care of yourself first, before you go take care of everybody else's to-do list (hello, email!), you will make a powerful shift mentally and physically, which will then set in motion a chain reaction of badassery. This means you will finally start getting done the things you want to. Maybe it's the weight you want to lose, or the nasty habit you need to quit, or the vacation you want to plan, or the certification you have got to start studying for.

A better life can be yours as soon as you are ready to start leveling up and change the soundtrack in your head to stop playing the "easy for her to say" song and start playing the "I deserve it" song.

World's Worst Boss

We are such jerks to ourselves, especially women. I mean would you *ever* work for someone who talked to you the way you talk to yourself? If the words in your head that you tell yourself about yourself were put on a billboard, would you be proud or embarrassed? The inner mean girl we all have is a total beeeyotch, and she needs to be shut down. Immediately. It's time to stop letting the freeloaders—things like anxiety, stress, fear, jealousy, and hate, which aren't paying any rent—live in your head any longer. If it doesn't serve you, if it keeps you stuck, if it makes you sick, it's time to kick them out.

Just image how life would change for you if you booted out these negative freeloaders and invited in more magical things like vulnerability, self-love, play, positivity, and trust; these things not only pay the rent on time—which is made in big deposits of health, energy, focus, confidence, and a sense of peace—but they also pay in advance for months that haven't even happened yet!

See, when you love yourself, you have no time for the freeloaders who pay no rent because you realize they are only there to trick you into believing you are not ready, worthy, or enough. It's time to kick them to the curb. You are enough, you were born ready, and you have more power than you realize.

You are enough, you were born ready, and you have more power than you realize.

No One Else Can Be You. This Is Your Power!

We all have moments when we quit on ourselves. In these moments we over-think, doubt ourselves, and decide that we are not good enough or worthy enough. For you, maybe it's the certification you "don't have time" to study for, the mammogram you keep putting off, the date you're not going on, the promotion you're not going for, the business you're not starting, or the bad habit you just can't seem to quit.

I wonder, What badass doors are you not opening because fear has you in a choke hold? What could the world possibly be missing out on because you are too afraid to level up?

I know a thing or two about being afraid to open doors.

Not a lot of people know that the very first time I signed up for improv classes at the Second City Training Center Conservatory in Chicago, I never even went. I paid the nonrefundable fee for the entire semester, left my apartment in Lincoln Park, and walked all the way to the training facility in Old Town. I even went into the building, up the stairs, down the hallway, and stood in front of my classroom door. But I never went in.

People saw me standing there and asked if I was lost or if I needed help.

I didn't want to tell them I was afraid, so I lied. I made up stuff like "My bad, I'm lost. Wrong room. Wrong class. Wrong day." I ran out of there with my tail between my legs.

Fear won that day. I was so stuck inside my head. I remember thinking, *I'm not good enough. I'm not smart enough. I'm not funny enough.* Oh, and I was the very "ancient" thirty years old at the time, so the main soundtrack in my head was: *I'm too old. It's too late. I'm too old. It's too late.* I assumed all these "kids" were trying to be on *Saturday Night Live*; what was I thinking?

So I quit; I gave up. And I regretted that decision for a long time.

Thank goodness I made a different choice about a year later. I signed up again for those classes at the Second City Training Center Conservatory, paid that nonrefundable fee again, and once again left my apartment in Lincoln Park and walked to the training facility in Old Town. I took a deep breath and went back into that building, walked up the stairs, down the hallway, and stood in front of my classroom door—but this time, this time I opened the door. The best part? When I opened that door, I saw people just like me. I even saw people older than me, like twenty years older. I'll never forget how it felt to prove that freeloader in my head wrong, the one telling me that I was "too old." Because right there in front of me was proof that I wasn't.

Opening that door, choosing courage over comfort, literally opened the door to the rest of my life—and certainly to my life as I now know it.

Improv at the Second City Training Center Conservatory really became my fear church, my fear yoga. It was where I went to get zen with my fear, by which I mean it's where I found peace with my fear. Because, you see, the more I did the scary thing onstage five, six, seven nights a week at the Second City Training Center Conservatory, the more I started to get the guts to do the scary thing on the stage of my life five, six, seven days a week. I started to get brave and bold and confident, and this confidence allowed me to open incredible doors, both personally and professionally.

At the time, I was working full-time in sales and marketing by day and studying improv at night. I started watching the things I was learning at the Second City Training Center Conservatory change the game for me onstage, so I thought: Why not try out some of these improv ideas at work and in my professional life? So I did! And doing this taught me that there is tremendous power in being brave enough to be exactly who you are.

No one else can be you. Only you can be you—this is your power. No one else does it your way. No one else was born with your special gifts and talents. No one else looks like you, walks like you, talks like you, eats like you, writes like you, dances like you, thinks like you, laughs like you.

No one else is you— this is your power.

When you really start trusting and believing that what you have is good enough, fear doesn't stand a chance.

TRUST YOURSELF

When you do improv, although you have to trust in your fellow improvisers onstage, you mostly have to trust in yourself. You have to trust that you bring a unique perspective to the stage that no one else has. That your story, physicality, ideas, and sense of humor are totally unique to you. This works in improv and in life, because we need, want, and crave that kind of variety in this world.

One of the first things I did to unlock my power was to start trusting myself. I mean *really* trusting myself. I had to trust that I *am* good enough and that what I have to offer matters. I started doing this in job interviews by asking more questions, on sales calls by not freaking out when things got quiet, in presentations by telling more authentic stories, around the board table by making others look good, with my senior leadership by asking for resources I needed, and even while dating by speaking up when I wasn't interested. All of this leads to less regret from day to day. I believe that what we really regret is our failure to speak up and protect our values when we have the chance to.

I started speaking up and asking for what I really wanted, which helped me sleep better at night and taught me the power of owning it. See, we need *you,* not a fake version of what you think we want you to be. You were born to stand out in this sit-down world; and the moment you realize that trust is the gateway drug to self-love, you step into your power.

We need you, not a fake version of what you think we want you to be.

WE NEED MORE PINK FLAMINGOS!

If you think of your work environment and industry right now, who are the pink flamingos? The people who stand out. The ones who seem to have an aura, an energy, and a vibe that you can't help but notice. The people who make you feel like you're the only one in the room when they talk with you. Mentally pause here, grab a pen and notebook, and write a list. Once you've gotten a few names down on paper, do you notice any patterns? Do they have anything in common? Are they doing any similar things?

The pink flamingos in your industry and in your company aren't only extroverts, or leaders, or a certain age. They aren't the ones with the most experience. They are the ones who have confidence and compassion, which fuel an energy you can't help but notice.

When you trust yourself and find power in your unique talents and perspectives, you'll become an example for others. You'll be a pink flamingo who refuses to let fear hold you back from finding ways to stand out among the flocks and flocks of boring ol' pigeons in this world.

It can be inspiring to watch someone be exactly who they are, without offering apologies for it. Growing up, I was obsessed with pink flamingos. I had a pink flamingo phone, a pink flamingo clock, pink flamingo bedding, pink flamingo stuffed animals, a pink flamingo calendar, pink flamingo school supplies. It was a pink flamingo explosion in my room and life. I'm not sure where this obsession came from exactly. Maybe it's because I grew up in St. Louis,

Missouri, in the middle of the American Midwest, and pink flamingos were rare, beautiful creatures I only got to see at the zoo.

Then I got to travel to Florida with my grade school BFF and her family, and got to see my first-ever pink flamingo in real life. Oh. My. God. My little teenage self was in awe. I remember standing against the railing looking at these beautiful pink birds, thinking, *Look at these flamingos, all tall and elegant and hot pink. They don't look like any of the other birds, and they don't seem to give one single "F" about it.*

It can be inspiring to watch someone be exactly who they are, without offering apologies for it.

Even now, I love what flamingos symbolize. They aren't afraid to stand tall, wear color, or stand out. They were born to stand out. So were you.

When we watch you truly be yourself, you become the pink flamingo in the room for us, and you will inspire others to want to do the same. We need you to give us more of who you are. We need you to be brave enough to love yourself. And we need you to have the courage to share your gifts with us.

Share the Love

Once you start loving yourself, you may feel vulnerable. However, it's a short-lived paradox. The world loves to tell you that loving yourself is conceited and self-absorbed. Think about it. You never hear anyone say things like "I woke up today, and I love myself so damn much." I mean, only a self-absorbed weirdo would say something so selfish and boastful, right?

Hell to the no!

Take, for example, Alex Toussaint, a Peloton instructor who is one of my favorite examples of positive self-love. He embraces this self-love and shares it with thousands of people every day. Peloton is a spin bike fitness craze that I'm 100 percent obsessed with. It's like having an indoor cycling studio in your house. I always say it's kind of like SoulCycle in your living room. Classes are live-streamed from their NYC studio or you can take them on demand. It's not only a killer workout, it's inspiring, motivational, and the instructors become like family.

In his classes, Alex says things like "Oh man, I feel so damn good today. I woke up today, and I love myself so damn much," and then he continues to sprinkle more "I love myself" comments into the ride.

When I first heard Alex do this during one of my rides, I found it refreshing and inspiring. It's uplifting to listen to someone so bravely tell thousands of riders all over the world how much he loves himself. He shows each of his students that it's okay to love yourself, and that when you do you will inspire others who want to embrace their own self-love and positivity to do the same.

Self-love is contagious, just like yawns and laughs are. You can't help but be in a good mood when you are around people who love themselves. Just like you can't stop laughing when someone else can't stop laughing. Self-love shifts focus from a fear-based "everything is going wrong" to a faith-based "everything is just as it should be."

There Is Nothing to Fix

Why is it that every time we look in the mirror we see only what needs to be fixed? We obsess over that new wrinkle, or the gray hairs that seem to come out of nowhere, or the fact that our nose isn't smaller, or that our eyebrows are too thin, or that our eyes aren't blue. We go through this mental checklist comparing ourselves to all the bullsh*t airbrushing we see online in social media. This makes you feel like crap. Like you aren't good enough, skinny enough, rich enough, smart enough, busy enough, or loved enough.

None of these things matter, and most of it is Photoshopped anyway. People aren't posting their crappy day or their cellulite or their bloated belly. In most cases, you are seeing only the highlight reel of someone else's life.

I want you to look into the mirror and start seeing your own highlight reel—with YOU being the highlight. I mean, look at you . . . you are alive! Your heart pumps blood through your body and beats more than one hundred thousand times a day so that you can walk around this beautiful earth. You have cells and molecules and organs and all kinds of other sciency stuff that allows you to travel, earn money, fall in love, eat good food, laugh, read this book right now, and oh yeah . . . breathe! I mean, we can't forget about that!

One simple shift I made to help me remember how good I have it is when I look in the mirror, instead of being upset about my reflection or finding my flaws, I think about how there is someone my age somewhere right now in a hospital on life support or very sick. Thinking of this unfortunate person reminds me that I'm not broken or ill. I'm here, alive—very much alive—healthy, and happy. These things are such a privilege. There is nothing to fix. There are only things to be grateful for.

There is nothing to fix. There are only things to be grateful for.

YOU AREN'T AN IMPOSTER

Do you ever have that feeling that one day everyone will discover that you are really a fraud? That you don't actually deserve your big job and even bigger salary? That you really have zero clue about what you're doing?

Hello, imposter syndrome. Welcome to the fear party. According to an article in *Harvard Business Review*:

> Imposter syndrome can be defined as a collection of feelings of inadequacy that persist despite evident success. "Imposters" suffer from chronic self-doubt and a sense of intellectual fraudulence that override any feelings of success or external proof of their competence. They seem unable to internalize their accomplishments, however successful they are in their field. High achieving, highly successful people often suffer, so imposter syndrome doesn't equate with low self-esteem or a lack of self-confidence. In fact, some researchers have linked it with perfectionism, especially in women and among academics.[1]

---

1   Gill Corkindale, "Overcoming Imposter Syndrome," *The Harvard Business Review*, May 7, 2008, https://hbr.org/2008/05/overcoming-imposter-syndrome.

I get this feeling all the time—hell, it's happening to me as I write these words. My fears are calling, saying, "What if everyone finds out you are not really a writer?"

Imposter syndrome is always asking "What if?" this and "What if?" that. It's an insanely destructive mental loop. It will knock you off your game if you aren't careful. And it's one of fear's favorite games to play.

I read that Maya Angelou once shared that each time she published a book, she thought, "Uh-oh, they're going to find out now. I've run a game on everybody, and they're going to find me out."[2]

If Maya-freaking-Angelou, one of the most legendary badass writers and thinkers of all time, dealt with this feeling, then yes, you are totally normal to be feeling it too. You are not alone. The way I look at it, when imposter syndrome arrives in your life, it shows that you are leveling up—and this growing process feels scary. Fear invites imposter syndrome to the party to stop you from leveling up, and to make you doubt everything, in hopes of stopping you from being the badass you are destined to be.

Guess what. NO ONE knows what they are doing most days! Growth is insanely uncomfy. When you are becoming a version of yourself you've never been before, it is scary as hell. When you earn that degree, get that promotion, land the big job, make more money, write the book, or enter the new relationship, you are entering unchartered waters. Give yourself some grace and take a deep breath.

You will feel awkward from time to time because it IS awkward when you do stuff you've never done. Who cares? Entering those new waters is success in itself. So go ahead and own it. You didn't get lucky by chance; you earned it.

It's okay to own your successes.
You didn't get lucky by chance.

---

2   As quoted in Margie Warrell's "Afraid of Being 'Found Out'? How to Overcome Impostor Syndrome," *Forbes*, Apr. 3, 2014, https://www.forbes.com/sites/margiewarrell/2014/04/03/impostor-syndrome/#7c8d97ab48a9.

Showing up is what matters the most, and it's also the hardest part, especially when you live in constant fear of being "found out." Doing it anyway—that's where you'll find your power. It's up to you to stop fear in its tracks and refuse to let your doubts dictate your choices.

EXCUSES ARE BS STORIES WE TELL OURSELVES

If there are two things that love each other more than anything, they're fear and excuses. Fear uses excuses to keep you stuck, safe, and just the same. Fear loves this stuckness because fear does NOT want you to level up. As a result, fear invites his old reliable friend excuses to join him at the party so that you feel extra safe in your choice to not boss up. Well, it's all BS. Excuses are a mind trick that fear uses to block you.

Maybe you have a fitness goal, a bad habit you need to quit, a toxic relationship you won't leave, a promotion you're not going for, or a business you're not starting . . . I'd bet my bottom dollar that nine times out of ten, what's on the other side of you not doing the thing you really want to do are a bunch of BS stories you keep telling yourself to make yourself feel better about not doing the thing you know you need to do.

In the years leading up to my eventually quitting my full-time job to write and speak full-time, I had so many excuses that kept me stuck in a job I hated. Excuses like "Next year I'll have more time and money," "I have no idea how to set up a website," "I don't want to let my boss down," "I'm not smart enough to run a business"—on and on and on it went. This constant loop of BS excuses kept me from making any kind of move. I stayed stuck and safe—and miserable.

During this time, I would attend conference after conference, watch the amazing speakers onstage, and think, *Why am I not up there? Why them and not me? It's not fair.* Then it hit me: the only person in my way was myself and the long list of excuses fear was using to stop me. Real bosses realize things are always happening FOR them and not TO them. This shift snaps them out of the victim mentality and right into reality.

When you realize that fear and excuses are BFFs,
you will start to regain your power and
have the courage to take one small first step.

When you realize that fear and excuses are BFFs, you will start to regain your power and have the courage to take one small first step. Maybe that first step is writing a list of people equally as amazing as you are who have figured it out so you gain confidence. Maybe the first step is hiring a coach to help you. Maybe you can read a how-to book by someone who has done the thing you seek to do. You could also watch a YouTube tutorial or phone a friend.

All it takes is one small first step. We don't need you to run the marathon yet; we simply need you to sign up for the race.

ON PROCRASTINATION

The problem is . . . we wait. For the perfect time, the perfect age, the perfect day. Fear loves when you procrastinate because it keeps you stuck and insecure. The perfect time to do anything is always right now. Doing the work matters.

The other day I needed to start creating a new half-day workshop for a client. I was on a deadline and this needed to get done like yesterday. But this workshop was new, something I've never done before. I wanted to do anything but sit down and do the actual work. Instead of getting the workshop started, I organized all these papers on my desk. And then you know what I thought? *Why not just go grab the cleaning spray, so I can wipe this desk down while I'm at it!*

Next thing I know it's been two hours. I had a sparkly clean office but not one damn word was written. I had done zero work. I could have cleaned my office anytime . . . later that night or on Saturday. But I was scared. I was scared to do the work because . . . *What if I suck? What if I'm in over my head on this one?*

What if what if what if.

It's so easy to slip into this bad habit. The only way you can stop procrastination is with action. So I set a timer for ten minutes and made myself do just ten minutes of work on the workshop. When the timer went off, I could either stop or keep going if I'd caught a vibe and felt inspired. Then I'd do it again the next day and the next day. It broke the big scary thing I had to do down into manageable time chunks, which created momentum instead of what-ifs. Before I knew it, I had an outline, and most days those ten-minute time chunks turned into an hour because that momentum gave me the motivation to keep going.

What do you keep putting off? Whether it's a workout, a project, or a phone call, all you need is ten minutes. This will be enough to get you going. Before you know it, you'll make progress and have momentum to carry you through.

The only way you can stop procrastination is with action.

Sh*t Happens

It's not all roses and daisies. For all the amazing things that you'll experience in life, you'll have just as many tough moments. I often feel as though life is like a roller coaster. Most of the time it's flashing along—super fast, and fun, and my hair is blowing in the wind, and I'm screaming, "HELL YES!" Yet in the back of my mind I'm waiting for the drop, the plummet, the moment my breath gets taken away; and I hate that part of the roller coaster.

You must brace yourself for the tough stuff. No one gets out of this life alive. Each of us will feel pain, sadness, and hurt. Yet when you love yourself, while you may lose your breath when that roller coaster drops, you know you'll be okay. You have built a foundation that is solid, and you know that no matter what, you are exactly where you are meant to be.

HURT PEOPLE HURT PEOPLE

One of the ideas that gives me grace when I'm dealing with people who've hurt me is the idea that only hurt people hurt people. It's as simple as that. People who hurt others emotionally, physically, and/or mentally do not love themselves. This is one of the most destructive side effects of not loving yourself.

I grew up in a pretty chaotic environment. We had the highest of highs and the lowest of lows. I have happy memories of parties with family friends, family BBQs at the park, and love-filled vacations to Minnesota. I also have equally strong memories of screaming, fighting, and crying. Especially when it came to my mom, who is mentally unstable; you never knew which version of her you were going to get. It could go from everything is all good, let's go shopping . . . to . . . *Duck!* as plates, lamps, and whatever else she could get her hands on were being thrown against the walls.

We once sat down for a classic 1980s summer dinner of KFC, only to have Mom go around the table in a rage dumping the food, one by one, over my and my siblings' heads. I was about eight years old at the time—old enough to know that wasn't what love should feel like. Yet, like most kids who grew up similarly, I didn't even realize there was another way.

My mother doesn't know how to really love because she probably had no love role models of her own. So she did the best she could with what she knew. I know that her past, her hurt, and her inability to deal with it all have kept her stuck. She won't travel, has never seen the ocean, has few interactions with family; most days, she's barely getting by. This makes me feel sad for her, but it also gives me the ability to express grace toward her. The grace to realize that for all the pain I feel about things in my past, I have to equally say thank you for them, because these experiences have made me who I am.

Grace can give you a healthy perspective when you get hurt by someone. Yet boundaries still matter. Grace isn't a hall pass; it doesn't condone sh*tty behavior in the person who got hurt. You have to protect your light with your life. But grace will allow you to move forward and turn the bad stuff into fuel for your fire. I look at it this way: I work hard as hell on myself; I work hard as hell to love myself and lift up others; and I put in the work to be the best version of myself every damn day. So why would I allow someone who does not put in the work and someone who does not love themselves to kill my vibe? I won't. No way—not happening. I will not tolerate manipulative people, even if they are someone in my family. You shouldn't either.

You can be a victim or you can be a badass.
The choice is yours.

Let me tell you: happy people do exist. I'm one of them. This doesn't mean I don't have my bad days. Lord knows I do, but most of the time I'm happy as hell. And because of this, I don't have time to hurt anyone else. I'm too damn busy being happy. And here's my favorite part: you can come from a sh*tty situation and still break the cycle; it's totally up to you. You can be a victim or you can be a badass. The choice is yours. You have to decide what you are willing to tolerate. And when you love yourself, this threshold is low—and it should be. While you can't escape bad stuff from happening, you can escape the mental jail it tries to put you in by simply loving yourself first.

ON GHOSTING

Ghosting is an abrupt end of a relationship with little or no warning at all. When you level up professionally, people may ghost you, exiting your life because your success makes them jealous. When you go through something traumatic like a diagnosis, divorce, or loss, people may ghost on you because your issue holds a mirror up to something they are afraid to face themselves. The common denominator here is that the reason they are ghosting is within themselves, not because of anything you did. When someone ghosts you, it's almost always because there is something they see in your circumstance that triggers something they are not ready to handle yet themselves.

When I first quit smoking, a few people at work would not hang out with me as much. It wasn't just that we were no longer "smoking buddies," but that this new version of me held up a mirror of what they could not yet do for themselves. It was way easier for them to ghost our friendship than to quit the nasty habit.

Additionally, I've had friends not attend a funeral to support someone they love because they either were afraid of that same loss happening in their own life or didn't know how to handle the trauma of the situation.

Maybe it's a divorce, and you lose friends because they don't know how to pick sides. Maybe it's a big promotion you make at work, and all of a sudden you are no longer invited out for lunch by work colleagues who now report to you. Maybe it's finally falling in love, and you lose friends because you no longer like going out to the bars every weekend. No matter how you slice and dice it, people will ghost. People will disappoint you. People will get scared.

It takes guts to counsel someone through a divorce while also trying to see both sides. It takes courage to help a friend beat a disease and visit them in the hospital. It takes grit to walk through the fire with someone who has just lost someone they love, and to hold their hand at the funeral. It takes commitment to love a friend when they change and grow into a better version of themselves.

As you get stronger in your love for yourself, these acts of fear by people you love will hurt less. You will realize people are flawed and scared and not perfect. You must be okay with the fact that you could lose some relationships along the way and that people may ghost you.

Bless them and move on. Because, FearBoss, you've got work to do.

A DATE WITH DISAPPOINTMENT

Disappointment is inevitable. Not only being disappointed but also disappointing others. People will let you down and break your heart. Yet the flip side is also true: you may let people down and may break a heart or two yourself. You cannot let this hold you back from pushing forward on your goals. Especially as a high achiever, you will need to have tough conversations with people you love. You may have to fire someone or set boundaries with a client. You may even try out a new initiative at work that totally flops or invest a bunch of money into this new business venture, only to find out it wasn't what you thought it would be. You will let people down and people will let you down; but you cannot allow this to hijack your focus and make you give up.

One of the hardest non-job jobs I've ever had was being chapter president of an association in the meetings industry. Although it was one of the proudest moments of my career, it was equally one of the most disappointing. I started to see how destructive ego and politics and agendas could be. So many people I loved let me down when I needed them the most. I started feeling like I couldn't trust anyone, including myself, which made me a different kind of leader. I wanted to hide and play it safe. I wanted to quit, multiple times. I wanted to tell everyone to eat a suck-it sandwich and ride off into the sunset. I wanted things to be how they "used to be." Before the egos, and the agendas, and the politics.

What saved me was not only the badass tribe I had cheering me on in that association, but also my relationship with fear. I knew fear wanted me to quit. I knew fear wanted me to take the easy way out. I knew fear wanted to keep me playing small. Fear wanted the negativity to win. But I had to keep going. You see, it's not supposed to be easy all the time, and the only way to grow is by getting uncomfortable and choosing courage. And boy, was I uncomfortable! But I was also growing. It's in feeling discomfort that you start to become who you really are.

There are so many people counting on you. Yes, it will get hard and people will let you down—someone may even break your heart. But you have to keep going. We need you: your perspective, your gifts, your talents, your leadership. When you push through, you give yourself such a gift: resilience. You may get knocked down, but dammit, you'll get up again.

In Conclusion

If you don't love yourself, the rest of the ideas in this book can't happen for you. You can't make fear your homeboy and also hate yourself. It's physically impossible. When fear is your homeboy, you love yourself so damn much you feel like Kate Winslet in that scene with Leo on the front of the *Titanic*, hair blowing in the wind, eyes closed, feeling all the feels and loving your damn life. Why? Because you are alive. Right now. And what a privilege that is! The question is: Are you ready to trust the universe?

How to Make Fear Your Homeboy
AND LOVE YOURSELF LIKE A #FEARBOSS:

1. Accomplish one thing for yourself at the beginning of the day.

Instead of checking your email first thing, why not check in with yourself? Start your day doing something for you first, *before* you pick up your phone or jump into work. For most of us, mornings are the most stressful. Here are a few ideas you can squeeze into your morning routine:

· Listen to a podcast while getting ready.

· Listen to an audiobook on the way to work or school drop-off.

· Take ten minutes and read ten pages of a book.

· Read a devotional or other form of inspiration.

· Write in a journal for ten minutes.

· Grab a cup of coffee and organize your day.

· Walk the dog.

You don't need an hour; all you need is to do one thing for *you* that will advance your life or your day before you start taking care of the rest of the world.

2. Create a Love Yo'self Mantra.

Take some time to pen a business or life mantra for yourself. For example: I have a biz mantra that reads "The universe is abundant and there is enough for all of us!" It reduces my anxiety and helps me think with an abundance mindset. One of my life mantras is "She believed she could, so she did." This reminds me to monitor my self-talk and silence my inner "mean girl" so I can keep moving forward. Craft a statement or two that works for you and post it somewhere visible. Bedroom mirrors, laptops, car dashboards, bathroom mirrors, or desktop computers are perfect places for these powerful affirmations. You want to look at it daily.

3. Ask how you would recover if something went wrong (and who could help you).

Listen, things will go wrong. It's a part of life. Yet often we get so caught up in the stuff that could go wrong, we forget that everything can be figured out. So if there is something worrying you, make a list of all the stuff that is worrying you about this particular "thing" you want to do or accomplish. Next to each item, on the right side, describe how you'd recover from each scenario, who could help you, and my favorite, has anyone less amazing than you figured it out?

4. Travel alone once a year.

Disconnect at least once a year and just be with yourself—even if it's taking one day and booking a cute B&B a mile from your house. Being alone forces you to learn what you are capable of, and knowing yourself leads to loving yourself.

5. Put one thing you love, or miss, on your schedule every week.

Maybe it's going to a concert, running errands without kids, brunch with the girls, reading a book in a park, a date with your main squeeze, a bubble bath, going to the movies. Whatever. Do you!

Don't forget to share your #FearIsMyHomeboy moments on social! Tag me and use the hashtag when you make any of these boss moves. I want to celebrate with you!

CHAPTER 2

The Universe Has Your Back

"Your life is always speaking to you.
The fundamental spiritual question is: Will you listen?"
—OPRAH WINFREY

In the summer of 2009, I witnessed a moment that forever changed the course of my life when I got to watch Simon Sinek speak. He was the headline keynote at an annual conference I was attending. Simon was there to present ideas from his book *Start with Why*. So there he was, larger than life onstage and projected onto huge dual screen monitors in front of almost four thousand of us. He was delivering a killer keynote, and I was hanging on to his every word.

Then about fifteen minutes into the speech, he stopped. He moved from center stage over to the lectern, shuffled some papers, took a drink of water, and wiped his brow. This lasted for several seconds. The audience began to stir, wondering what the heck was going on—myself included. *What was he up to?* Then, as the silence dragged on, I thought, *Wait, does he need a medic?*

Then, Simon looked up and said, "Ladies and gentlemen, I'm so sorry. I'm a little embarrassed—and I've never done this before—but I've gotten off track and lost my place. I'm so sorry."

You could feel the audience holding their breath. Poor Simon had just blanked out, everyone's greatest fear about public speaking, and he did it in front of thousands of people. It could have been a disaster, but instead it became a gift.

He paused, looked right at all of us, and then said, "However, it is in this moment, right here right now, I have never been more sure or reminded that I am alive!" He went on, "My hands are shaking, my heart is racing, and my blood is pumping like crazy, but ladies and gentlemen, I am very much alive."

It was a moment of raw vulnerability. Simon admitted his fear, and in doing so, he showed us that even though he was the keynote speaker, he was also just like the rest of us. One by one, we rose to our feet and gave this man a mid-keynote standing ovation to let him know we saw him and that we were moved by his raw vulnerability.

Of course, he got back on track and went on to deliver the rest of his keynote, and received another, and much deserved, standing ovation. But what Simon gave us was so much more than his keynote: he literally showed us what it looks like to *feel* your fear and move forward anyway, to trust the process and *yourself* so damn much you know that no matter what, you've got this. *That's* what it means to make fear your homeboy; you can take a moment of fear and turn it into a gift.

No Mistakes, Only Gifts

When you trust yourself and the process, it gives you the courage to lean into new opportunities that are outside your comfy zone, like speaking onstage, asking for a promotion, or speaking up in a meeting, because you know you will be okay—even if you fail, or bomb, or mess up. In fact, these "mistakes" are opportunities for growth.

Let's first talk about "trusting the process" and what that means. This was a big lesson I learned while doing improv. Though improvisers seem to be "making it up as they go," they are actually using their training to succeed onstage. Improvisers make it look easy, and constantly give the audience moments where they wonder, "How do they do that?"

The answer is: improvisers have been trained, first and foremost, to trust the process. Here, "process" means: "No mistakes, only gifts." If something unexpected happens onstage, your training will help you transform it into something fun for you and the audience. This idea can set you free. Because when you know that it's okay to mess up, and actually that "messing up" is required training in order to become even more badass at the thing you want to do, you slice through your fear, and realize that each time you struggle you are actually growing.

Look at Simon. He was doing something scary, speaking onstage in front of all those people. That is a brave endeavor in itself. Yet, that's not even the icing on the fear cake. The icing is the moment he decided to trust and love himself enough to get through the "blanking out" moment onstage. Simon was improvising up there. He messed up, made a "mistake," and instead of giving up, he turned that into a magical display of self-love, trust, and authentic vulnerability.

What if he had run off the stage because he couldn't handle it? Imagine if he decided the world didn't need another keynote speaker, so he stayed safe in his NYC apartment and just wrote. Imagine if Simon never even wrote *Start with Why* to inspire the rest of us. Think of all the things that would be missed out on because Simon chose fear over courage. Because he wrote that book, because he spoke on that stage, and because he kept going even when he lost his place, he changed the world. I mean, look, Simon's story from that day made it into this book; it certainly changed my life, and now I've shared that story with you!

Watching someone do the scary thing, and prevail, creates a ripple effect of inspiration. According to a study reported in the *Harvard Business Review:*

> The neuroscience shows that recognition has the largest effect on trust when it occurs immediately after a goal has been met, when it comes from peers, and when it's tangible, unexpected, personal, and public. Public recognition not only uses the power of the crowd to celebrate successes, but also inspires others to aim for excellence. And it gives top performers a forum for sharing best practices, so others can learn from them.[3]

Every time you choose courage over comfort, you are changing the world. You become a bravery role model. When we watch you do the scary thing

---

3   Paul J. Zak, "The Neuroscience of Trust," *The Harvard Business Review*, Jan.-Feb. 2017,
     https://hbr.org/2017/01/the-neuroscience-of-trust.

and prevail, it not only makes us trust you more, it gives us hope that we can do the scary thing and prevail in our own lives too. Fear is contagious. So is courage.

YOU'RE AN IMPROVISER

Let me bust out the HOLLA dictionary. I define improv as: "Two or more people collaborating in environments of uncertainty with the common goal of creating a solution." I bet you are doing these things every day. At work, you're creating solutions for your clients. At home, even getting your kids out the door with pants on is a massive accomplishment. And, you're negotiating with your significant other and coworkers constantly. You are compromising and collaborating all the time with zero script. You, my friend, are an improviser.

You are compromising and collaborating all the time with zero script. You, my friend, are an improviser.

The improvisational mindset is one of discovery, and it can help you stay focused. Using this perspective, you stay curious and in forward motion. In improv, it's not about the *best* thing, it's about the *next* thing. Momentum is everything and contribution is king. So if you're speaking up in meetings or teaching your team new things—that's improv!!

Additionally, improvisers are able to quickly switch their lens and see circumstances in different ways. Improvisers don't see obstacles, we see opportunities. Improvisers don't see change as an interruption but as an exciting introduction to what's next.

This mindset could empower you: when you see change and disruption as an exciting plot twist rather than something scary and unknown, you step into your power and open the door to staying relevant because you have faith that change is fuel, not something to fear.

Fear Can't Stand with Faith

Remember doing "trust falls" as kids? God, I hated them. That plank we'd walk out onto felt as tall as the Empire State Building, and looking back down at your grade-school friends (who weighed no more than a collective one hundred pounds and included a few kids who didn't even like you), you had no idea if this was going to work out. But the teacher made you do it, and you didn't want to look like a total wuss, so you closed your eyes, tried not to pee yourself, and fell back.

This was a moment of leveling up. It was a moment where you had to trust in your friends and classmates—yes—but it's also a moment when you demonstrated the power of trusting yourself first. You put yourself in an uncomfortable position with only the hope that it would work out, and you did this because you hoped that no matter what happened, you'd be okay. That jump, even when you're scared, *that's* faith.

That jump, even when you're scared, that's faith.

The other kids would catch you and then there'd be high fives, hugs, laughs, smiles, and mad endorphins. This magic is what it's like every time you do the thing you think you can't. It's what comes when you put your trust, and your faith, in yourself—not fear.

When I give keynotes, I ask for volunteers to come onstage with me and improvise. These people are brave, yet they are also faced with fear. My guests start out afraid, trembling with fear, and then two minutes into the scene onstage they are making the entire room laugh hysterically and end up getting ravenous applause.

Ninety-nine percent of the time when I do this with someone, the person who volunteered looks at me after the scene has ended, while the audience is applauding, and goes, "That was awesome!!" That attitude shows the magic of faith. Because the volunteer had *faith* in themselves that they could work with me to do the improv scene onstage, they made the choice to volunteer. It's in these moments you really see what people are made of.

Fear doesn't want you to raise your hand and volunteer to come onstage with me and improvise. Fear doesn't want you to level up and go for that promotion. Fear does not want you to lead the next breakout at your industry conference or run the next sales meeting in your office. Fear does not want you to quit smoking or leave the crappy relationship. The second you have faith that you could make these choices or changes and get closer to happiness, fear throws a fit. Fear likes you hanging out with him all nice and comfy on the couch watching reruns of *Say Yes to the Dress*.

When you trust yourself and the process, faith joins the fear party. Fear can't stand with faith. Faith is way too strong.

Fear can't stand with faith. Faith is way too strong.

The "What If" Syndrome

Fear loves being a DJ—he's damn good at it, too. He'll spin tracks all day thinking he's Dr. Dre, and the worst part is that he never takes a day off. *"Who the hell do you think you are?"* was the soundtrack that fear put in my head on repeat the second I got my book deal.

Fear doesn't want you to trust, and he definitely doesn't want you to level up. He wants to keep you safe—and exactly the same place you are now.

The day I got assigned my editor for this book was magical, but also scary. Even though my publisher told me we'd be a great fit, the fact that we were about to start working together meant sh*t was about to get real. *Who the hell do you think you are?* Fear played in my brain. Gulp. And then I saw she was a PhD. Record scrraaaaaaaatch. There it went again: *Who the hell do you think you are? She is this badass PhD—and what are you? What if she thinks I'm dumb or doesn't want to take on this project?*

I got writer's block before I could even write a word. I even sent her an email saying I changed my mind, that I was rethinking this book. What if instead of a *book* book we do more of a coffee-table workbook-type book? Isn't that way more "safe"?

We had a call shortly after and she gently told me that while my new idea was cool and fun for another time, *this* book was what I needed to be working on. I needed to trust the knowledge I had about befriending fear and also trust that I really am an expert on this. Boom. She shook me right out of my fear funk and woke me up to what I was doing to myself. Welcome to the party, "what if" syndrome.

This is one of fear's favorite tactics in getting you off track. That's exactly what I did when I got all in my head about working with my editor. *What if this . . . what if that.* You can do this all day every day, by the way, and never get a real answer—because there never is one. You have *zero* clue what the future will hold. All you can be responsible for is *right now,* and your choices in this moment. These small choices eventually will determine your destiny.

· What if I get fired? You'll use your badassery to get another job.

· What if he leaves me? You'll end up with the love you deserve.

· What if I don't get the promotion? You'll find another opportunity you never saw coming.

· What if they make fun of me? They already are, so why not give them something to talk about?

· What if I embarrass myself? What a great story you'll have!

· What if I don't pass the certification test? You'll try again.

Do you see a pattern here? Each "what if" scenario tries to block you from leveling up.

Each "what if" scenario tries to block you from leveling up.

The last time I checked, no one got anywhere great without having to dip their toes into the holy-crap-this-is-scary pond from time to time. All of the what-ifs and BS stories living in your head have one job: to stop you from leveling up. When you have faith in yourself and trust that the universe always has your back, you can step out of fear and into who you were designed to be.

Invite a Friend to the Fear Party

Have you ever signed up for a networking event, luncheon, or industry function and the second you find out that someone you know will be there, you jump for joy? You think, *Oh thank God, yes, now I will know someone . . . this won't be so bad after all!* That is what it feels like to have a friend come along to the fear party.

If you want to level up, you can't just sit around doing what you've always done. You have to trust-fall into new people, places, opportunities, and experiences. Bringing a friend, something or someone you know and trust, with you to the fear party is a badass way to make the scary thing a little less overwhelming.

If you need to give a big presentation, start with a story. This will help you connect with the audience and make you feel more comfortable onstage. The story is your friend. If you're going for a big promotion, read through rave reviews from happy customers and colleagues right before you go in (even better, print them out and bring them with you). These reminders are your friends in the room, giving you the confidence to crush it.

These friends can be anything that you trust. Maybe it's a piece of jewelry you wear, a book you keep with you, photos you carry, essential oils you use. Find things that make you feel comfortable and use them to make the scary thing a little more comfy. Every time I go to the dentist, I bring my rose-gold Beats and blast '90s gangster rap. This helps my anxiety and makes me feel super tough so I can get through it. The hip-hop is my friend at the scary-dentist fear party.

Find things that make you feel comfortable and use them to make the scary thing a little more comfy.

Scary things don't get less scary; you just get stronger. Bringing a friend to the fear party will help you work the room with confidence, clarity, and courage. You get to decide when fear is invited, and when it's not. Remember: this is your life party, and you get to call the shots.

Naming What You Want

If you don't know what you want, how can the universe, or anyone else, for that matter, help you get it? It can feel scary as hell to actually think, or speak out loud, the dreams, desires, and goals you have; but this is a critical piece in managing your fear. When you speak out loud, what is it that you want, you put it into motion.

Most of us don't speak or visualize our deepest desires because the biggest fear we have isn't death, or speaking in public, or failure—it's actually the fact that we may just succeed. So make it a part of your life to constantly be visualizing, talking about, and taking action on steps to get you closer to the things you want.

One of the most popular ways to name what you want is to have either a future board or some sort of journaling practice. There are no rules here on how this should look, because everyone has a different vibe. Based on who you are and how you roll, you may want to write down your dreams, goals, and desires in a journal every day. You may want to build a future board, something you look at every day. You may want to create a "where I'll be in five years" plan that you check in with annually. Maybe you do a combo of all the above! All of these ideas are right. All of them force you to focus on the future you, which is how you put what you actually want into motion.

Each of these rituals will give you the courage to tell the world what you want. I mean, the first time I spoke out loud that I would meet Oprah and/or speak at Super Soul Sunday, it felt insanely crazy. I got butterflies, even feeling a wave of panic, at the sheer power of the thought. Then I thought, *Why not me?*

And if I'm crazy enough to think it and say it, then maybe I'm crazy enough to actually do it! Thank you, universe, I'll just be hanging out right here by my phone waiting for Oprah to call. In the meantime, I'm gonna keep slapping Oprah pictures onto my future board.

This year I checked in on my "Judi in five years" plan that I wrote in 2013 (which meant it was time for a new one!), and I almost spit out my coffee. At the time, I had written down things that were so big I felt super uncomfortable: write a book, quit my job, marry Scott, triple my income, speak for a living, get standing ovations, be healthy, hire an admin, build a beautiful website, travel the world.

Guess what?

All of it happened, and is still happening! Five years ago, I set my intentions, and then took action day by day to advance each dream or goal. The future board helped me realize what I wanted, and it inspired me to start the work. This future-board practice helped me stop feeling lost and start getting focused.

As you work on your plan, think about the following questions and how they might look in your life:

- Do you dream of financial freedom?
- Do you want to lead a team?
- Would you like to work from home?
- Do you want love?
- Would you like to travel to Italy?
- Could you use a little more balance?
- Where do you dream of living?
- What do you dream of earning?
- How do you want to dress?
- How do you want to feel?

Developing a visualization practice gives you focus while also telling the universe what you want. Ask, Hustle, Receive. The formula works every time.

BOOMERANGS, YO!

Human energy is a boomerang: what you put out, you will get back. Kinda like karma. Which means you must be careful what you wish for—you may just get it. If you are constantly telling yourself you're miserable, lonely, broke, depressed, sick, and pissed off . . . you'll stay that way. Period.

If you put out negativity, you will get negative people, places, and things in your life. If you put out good vibes, more good may come to you. Now for a disclaimer: this does not mean sh*tty stuff doesn't happen to good people. We can't escape hard people and situations. Yet, when you tell the universe what you really want, you put good energy in motion. You open yourself up to it, and you start the process of remembering the improv mantra that there are "no mistakes, only gifts."

So speak it, write it, shout it, sing it, rap it—whatever feels most comfy for you. Tell a different story, one where you're safe, healthy, happy, brave, strong, and alive; even if you feel like crap, you'll start to strengthen your energy. This stronger energy will boomerang around, allowing these positive things to come into your life.

When you tell the universe what you really want, you put good energy in motion.

The boomerang came around for me when I started telling the universe, and the world, that I wanted to be onstage speaking. For years, I felt this path deep in my bones and knew it was what I needed to be doing with my life. I began putting myself out there on social media, slowly starting to build a brand and share my passion for speaking. These posts reminded my followers that I was for "hire" if anyone wanted to learn more about how improv could help them stand out and manage fear. I shared photos of me speaking, started a blog, built a website, and started teaching the ideas I share in my talks in bite-sized chunks via status updates and tweets.

I'll never forget getting booked for my first-ever real corporate client. A girl-friend from high school knew that I was starting to speak professionally because she followed me on social. My friend could easily show her boss my blog, my website, and my social feed to show him that I was passionate, experienced, and ready for hire. And her boss did! They paid me actual money to fly on a plane, stay in a hotel, and speak to their sales team of about a hundred people. Boomerang caught!

Later, as I flew home at night on a super-empty plane in a row all by myself, I cried like a baby. Overwhelming, happy tears of joy and amazement. *I did it. I really did it.* I asked for it, prayed for it, worked hard to get it, believed I could do it, seized an opportunity, and now I run a business doing this full-time. That was a boomerang I caught and haven't let go of.

Is there something calling you that you aren't listening to? Do you really, really want something, and wonder why you are not getting it? Ask for it. Show up every day for yourself. Believe in yourself and trust the universe. When you love yourself, show up, work hard, and believe that you can do it . . . you better watch out—because that boomerang will come smack you in the head when you least expect it.

A MINUTE ON MINDFULNESS

One thing that can help slow down your monkey mind, keep you healthy, and give you a platform for visualization is an activity called mindfulness. This idea used to scare the heck out of me. I assumed that mindful people were like these peaceful zen-filled white doves that floated around above all of us "normal people," because they had an ability to sit in silence for long periods of time.

Mindfulness felt like something I couldn't touch. That meant I avoided it. Yet now I realize that each one of us can practice it. And, contrary to what you may believe, mindfulness doesn't mean you have to sit down for a deep meditation practice, do yoga, or burn incense. You can do it anytime you want—in fact, without realizing it, you may be doing it already!

One day I was listening to Jenna Kutcher's *Goal Digger* podcast, and she explained that mindfulness simply means "intentional attention." Damn! This hit me to my core. This simple explanation of something I used to be so afraid of made me realize that it's not this big scary thing after all. In fact, I am mindful! A lot. Because intentional attention is what we do in improv! We are intentional about our attention—we are in the moment—in order to succeed onstage. This is being mindful.

You are being mindful every time you become aware of where your attention is. Every time you simply notice what you are doing, that's being mindful. You can practice mindfulness anywhere: on a spin bike, sitting on a plane, standing in line at the grocery store, or in your next conversation. The next time you're out with your friends, keep your phone in your purse, not on the table. This simple gesture is being intentional about the fact that your attention could be taken away and that you are choosing your friends over distractions. Next time you hop on the spin bike, remove your iWatch so you can't check the time or worry about the cals you're burning. This intentional attention allows you to really be in the room and instead focus on the privilege of being able to move your healthy body, because there are many who can't. Maybe it's the next time you check out at the grocery store, instead of rushing through the process you say hello to the cashier, look them in the eyes and actually smile, taking notice of all the healthy food you are able to buy, then say a quick prayer of thanks for all the food in your cart. This intentional attention will immediately give you a jolt of gratitude and keep you humble.

You are being mindful every time you become aware of where your attention is.

We have to look up. We have to stop. We have to be where we really are. Mindfulness will slow down the clock for you and make your life feel like all of a sudden it's being projected in high-def color. You will start to notice things you never did before about your surroundings, other people, and yourself, and this awareness will allow you to feel more peaceful and also more connected with others. You will start to reduce your anxiety because you are not letting your technology control you. You will become more memorable at networking events and build trust with your team, because people will feel like the only one in the room when they are with you.

You don't have to be a Yogi Buddha who does silent meditation retreats to be filled with zen—a state of feeling calm and connected. But don't overthink it. When you are intentional about your attention, you are being mindful.

Hustle Luck

The word *hustle* gets a bad rap. So let's go to Hustle School for a hot second and lean into the power of this word and what it really means.

HUSTLE IS NOT

· grinding twenty-four hours a day

· checking email on weekends

· skipping vacations

· thinking sleep is lazy

· saying yes all the time

HUSTLE IS

· doing less but doing it better, with more focus and clarity

· giving yourself time to take a break

· getting enough sleep

· scheduling priorities and seizing opportunities

· saying no with grace

We look at people who are crushing it, and we may feel envious or jealous. We think: *They are so lucky. They have it all! Must be nice to be so lucky.*

I've got news for you, #FearBoss. These people are not lucky at all—they are hustling. I believe the real definition of hustle is clearly defining where you want to go and then taking the steps necessary to get there.

Your hustle may look different from other people's, and it *should*, given that it has to be based on who you are and where you want to go. Your hustle will also change at different stages of your life. Who you are and what you want at twenty is a lot different from who you are and what you want at forty. Think about what you want to achieve. Do you want to lose weight? Then your hustle is cutting sugar, counting calories, and not ghosting the gym. Do you want to start a blog? Then your hustle is reading books on blogging, taking classes, and skipping brunch on Sundays so you can work on launching yours. Perhaps you want a promotion at work? Hustle on your brand at work by raising your hand to take on more projects, strike up conversations with leadership, and go for a certification.

When you understand what hustle really means, by default you can make yourself lucky too.

HUSTLE FOR JOY

The second we get stressed and overwhelmed, the first things we tend to cut are vacations, fun, eating well, working out, and all kinds of stuff that are actually the medicine we should be taking. You think that skipping brunch with the girls or ghosting the gym will give you precious time back so you can finally get "caught up"? Here's the hard truth: you will never be caught up. Stop putting yourself last to chase around everyone else's to-do list.

When you skip doing the things you love because you feel you don't have the time, you end up wasting time later and beating yourself up about it—and the only person you hurt is yourself! You NEED joy in your life. When you are happy personally, you thrive professionally. When you are happy at work, it positively impacts your personal life. They go together.

Hustle for joy first; then go take care of the rest of the world. We spend so much time at work, you might as well be happy there. And if you're a leader, it's your duty to make it a positive, encouraging, and FUN place to be. I know an organization that does "bar cart Fridays" and rolls a little happy hour into the office every Friday afternoon, which totally bonds the team. I also know an organization that converted an old meeting space into a "nap" room for employees to recharge in the afternoon; they're encouraged to take twenty-minute naps between two and four in the afternoon.

Stop breaking promises to yourself. Stop canceling and not doing the things you really want to do. Make time with friends, go on vacations, hit the gym, take walks, read books, and go to the park with your kids. Make this MANDATORY on your schedule. Get your spouse on board. Make it a thing. A non-negotiable thing.

While hustling for joy is the goal, you will have bad days and feel off from time to time. That's okay! No one can be happy every second of every day. But you can get close! Happy people do exist, and it's because they take their joy medicine on the regular. They hustle as hard for joy as they do at their actual job. They don't skip doses or try to find ways around it. Hustling for joy will help you feel more confident, powerful, and fulfilled—which is just what the world needs: more confident, powerful, and fulfilled badasses.

Hustle for joy first; then go take care of the rest of the world.

THERE IS ENOUGH FOR ALL OF US

It's so easy to hustle the wrong way because of fear. You get scared that time is running out and that you gotta get yours, and if you don't get it right-freaking-now, you'll miss your chance. So you rush and react and overwork to try and fit it all in. You keep others at bay and don't share "too much" for fear they may take what little you've got. Then you end up crabby, stressed out, sick, and alone. This scarcity mindset will only keep you stuck. You must know that the universe is abundant.

There is enough for all of us.

One thing all fear bosses have in common is operating with a mindset of abundance instead of scarcity. A fear boss believes "there is enough for all." They know that there is plenty of room for all of us. They embrace people who inspire them and actually seek them out. Fear bosses are constantly asking: What can I learn from this amazing person? What can I contribute? How can I help? What can I teach? Who can I connect with?

Take the abundance mindset and let it inspire you to lead differently, love differently, and give differently. You must only see your world through the eyes of possibility and positivity. Stop worrying about someone stealing your idea, and instead remember that no one can replicate the badassery that only you possess. The next time fear tells you that you have failed somehow because you haven't achieved as much as another person has, take a deep breath and remember that someone else's success is not your failure. If you're anxious that another person might get promoted instead of you, stop secretly hating that person and start studying what makes them stand out. You can do all of these things with a perspective of abundance. There is enough for all of us. No one can ever replicate who you are and how you do it.

Remember that someone else's success is not your failure.

THE SHOW MUST GO ON!

You may be surprised to know that improvisers are some of the most trustful non-trusting people you'll ever meet. Here's what I mean by this seemingly paradoxical description: we learn to trust our ensemble (fellow actors) and ourselves, but we also know sh*t could hit the fan at any time because we are making the improv scene up as we go. Knowing that everything could fall apart at any moment means we are ninja-like prepared. We use our training to prepare for the "holy shit" moments that could happen onstage, and this allows us to feel more comfortable doing the scary thing to begin with.

When you live in a world where anything can happen, preparation becomes your lifeline. We have a plan A, and then plans B, C, and D. I was once told that how much you rehearse means how much you respect your audience, and this is true outside of improv as well. Preparation is a huge part of bossing up, because preparation allows you to feel more comfortable doing the scary thing, which allows you to slay. Preparation shows your audience that you are a professional and that you mean business.

Have you ever been to a presentation when the salesperson or presenter just shows up and "wings it"? This person is unfocused; and because the content isn't organized, the audience ends up getting no value for their time. You should never wing it. Every time you do, you are saying to your audience, "I don't respect you." This, in turn, makes them not respect you.

I once gave a keynote in Florida where thirty seconds into my opening story I realized the AV team could not get my slides up. My slides are a big part of the visual storytelling I do onstage. As I knew this was unfolding, I felt myself getting frustrated and kind of panicking. I could see the AV guy offstage trying to recover the files, but I got the impression that it wasn't going to work. I was onstage with 800 people staring at me. Gulp. It was time to practice what I preach and welcome fear to my keynote party.

I gave my presentation without slides. I put my improv training to good use. As an improviser, I instantly thought "plot twist!" instead of "get me off this stage" when I figured out that I wasn't going to have the slides to support my talk. I saw this as a chance to grow, test my skills, and learn. I had practiced my talk so many times that I knew it well, and I was ready. My slides are mostly visual placeholders to the stories I tell and content I teach when I give a keynote, so I knew I could do it without them. In fact, I had even prepared a printed backup of my slide deck to serve as my loose script in case this exact thing happened.

If I hadn't prepared, rehearsed, trusted myself, and had a backup plan, it would have been an absolute disaster. Was I frustrated? Yes. Was I uncomfortable? Yes. Did I let it stop me? No. Did the audience know any different? No. Did I feel the fear and do it anyway? HELL YES!

You have no script, no guarantees in life. What do you have? The ability to prepare. Mentally, physically, and emotionally. This means that you can have a scary thing coming, and you get ready for the best- AND worst-case scenarios. You take practical steps to ensure that if something you might be able to prepare for happens, you can still perform. For example, you might do as I did and have a printed backup of your slides before giving a big presentation. Or, if you've got a scary doctor's appointment coming up, you could plan for both positive and negative outcomes. You could envision it going well yet also run through unpleasant scenarios with a friend so there's a plan for how things could go during your recovery. In each scenario, you are making it up as you go, but you are also as prepared as you can be for the situation at hand.

There will be chaos in life. Shit will hit the fan. You could lose your job, or not get a promotion. You could get dumped. But even if these things happen, you will be okay. Why? You are prepared.

It is a whole lot easier to trust the process, and have faith in yourself, when you are prepared for the best- and the worst-case scenarios.

How to Make Fear Your Homeboy
AND TRUST THE UNIVERSE LIKE A #FEARBOSS:

1. Implement a "power statement" practice.

Start your day by grabbing a notebook and writing down ten power statements you either believe to be true about yourself, or wish to be true about yourself. A few of my personal favorites are: *I am healthy. I am wealthy. I am not anxious. I work with Fortune 100 companies. I fly only first class. I am creative.* While some are true and some aren't, don't limit yourself—because when you do, you end up becoming limited. Dream big here, think big here. There are no limits to what you can wish for and dream for yourself. Then, once you get them down on paper, read them to yourself and speak them aloud every day.

2. Create a visualization practice.

Visualization techniques have been used by high achievers for ages. They can help you create your dream life by accomplishing one task or goal at a time with laser focus and confidence. When you create a future board, journal, or develop a "me in five years" plan, you will build internal motivation, fire up the law of attraction, and reprogram your brain so you are ready to recognize the resources and opportunities needed to achieve your goals. Visualization allows you to change your beliefs and assumptions about yourself.

3. Build a God box.

In the book *Outrageous Openness: Letting the Divine Take the Lead*, author Tosha Silver suggests using a "God box" to help with anxiety, and turn over worry to the Divine.

Write down all the stuff you are worried about, personally and professionally, and pop it into some kind of container, as simple or fancy as you want. Whenever a new worry comes up, into the God box it goes. "I'll never find love"—into the God box. "What if we don't get the house?"—into the God box. "Will I ever get the raise?"—into the God box. "I'm too old"—into the God box.

Trust that worry to your higher power. Say to yourself, "It's in the box . . . it's handled."

This doesn't mean you put it in the box and then do nothing. You still have to show up and do the work to advance your dreams, goals, and desires . . . yet you have to trust that it's already handled, and that your life is unfolding just as it should. Stressing, fearing, and having anxiety over the unknown is a waste of your time and energy.

4. Save encouraging email in a snaps folder (as in finger "snaps" instead of hand "claps").

Anytime you get an email from a happy client, customer, or member of your community that says something encouraging about you, or your work, save it in a single folder.

Later, the second you fill with self-doubt, want to quit, or "what if" yourself into imposter syndrome, open this folder up. You'll quickly be reminded of how badass you are and that your work matters.

5. Throw a mistake party.

At work, when a mistake happens or there is a failure of some sort, instead of letting it linger and fester negativity around the office, why not throw a party for it and turn it into a powerful learning opportunity where you literally unwrap all the gifts the "mistake" gave your company, or your team?

How to throw a mistake party:

1. A "mistake" happens, like losing an account or not making a goal.

2. Someone on your team books a conference room.

3. Said conference room gets decorated with a few balloons or confetti sprinkled on the conference table to set the vibe.

4. Flip charts are arranged, or there is a whiteboard in the room.

5. Team gathers in the conference room.

6. Mistake party starts!

   · Start unwrapping all the unseen gifts the loss, mistake, or failure brought about.

   · Ask questions like: What did we learn? How can we improve next time? What good came out of it? How did we grow?

   · Have someone record your findings so you can share with those not present and have a record of the conversation to reflect on.

   This will send a powerful message about the power of positivity and allow you to remain in control, rather than caving in to the fear of failure.

   Don't forget to share your #FearIsMyHomeboy moments on social! Tag me and use the hashtag when you make any of these boss moves. I want to celebrate with you!

CHAPTER 3

Balanced by Design

"You are one decision away from a completely different life."
—MEL ROBBINS

I t's time to boss up and get to work on how you prioritize yourself in your life. Fear loves to make you feel guilty for putting time for yourself into your schedule. Fear will trick you into thinking you are selfish, that you'll get fired if you take time off or don't check email first thing; but this is all total BS. The BEST thing you can do for your career, your family, and your health is to make YOURSELF a priority.

Yet we now live in a culture that is moving at the speed of light and "crazy busy" is glorified. It's almost like being stressed out is a badge of honor. Really, it's more like a badge of crazy. I don't want you to feel crazy or stressed out any longer. I want you to thrive!

When you are not thriving personally, things won't work as well professionally. And when you are miserable professionally, you are affected personally. Each scenario shows up in all kinds of ways.

Let's take scenario #1: you are not thriving personally. This affects your career in countless ways. You lack confidence, which causes you to hold back more, so you don't go for the promotion or raise. You are overwhelmed trying to do "everything," and you start dropping balls, which makes you seem unreliable, which then affects your reputation. If you're feeling exhausted, you may not take on new projects or initiate as much. You definitely don't move outside your comfort zone like you used to when you were feeling more joy in your life.

Now, let's look at scenario #2: you are miserable at work. Again, this shows up in multiple ways in your personal life. You might take out your negative feelings on your spouse/partner or friends and family. You could end up canceling plans with others because you feel stressed and overwhelmed. Your health could suffer, too, if you keep ghosting the gym or eating fast food because you don't have time to cook.

The antidote to both of these scenarios is balance. By this I mean straight-up balance—not the so-called work-life balance we hear so much about. Because the reality is, I don't believe there is such a thing as work-life balance; there's no point in separating work from life. Work is a part of your life, and it's literally HOW you afford to live. So naturally your life is affected by your work. And who you are as a person is deeply affected by the environment you work in every day. Think of how many hours you spend working each week—in some cases we're at work more than we're at home. The positives and negatives of what you do are bound to bleed into your personal life. True balance requires understanding trade-offs, at work and in life. There is always a trade-off. Always.

I don't believe there is such a thing as work-life balance; there's no point in separating work from life.

The solution is balance. And balance is the foundation to your freedom. We all want more freedom in our lives. The freedom to work on a project and be fully focused because we've designed our schedule to be that way; the freedom to be present when you are with friends, family, and/or clients because we've removed distractions and built this time into our schedule; and the freedom to take the day off because we've built a buffer into our schedule that allows us to be spontaneous.

This freedom, however, requires you to be brave enough to protect your time. It means you must design a schedule that allows you to be focused, present, and spontaneous. We want to work at places filled with people who understand real balance, because this gives us the freedom to do work we love while feeling fulfilled personally. Sometimes fear keeps you stuck doing the same things you've always done because you assume it will never work, and that "balance" is for other people who have cool jobs. So you stay nice and safe and miserable running on the hamster wheel of overwhelm. #FearBoss, it's time to stop the madness and fix your list!

Fix Your List

Right now I want you to grab a blank piece of paper and a pen. I'll wait. Okay, you got it?[4]

Now, when I say *go*, I want you to take two minutes and list the things that are most important to you right now. These could be people, places, projects, goals, dreams, or material possessions. There are no rules for what needs to be on the list, other than it has to be important to you. Okay, the clock starts now. Two minutes—GO!

(Two minutes later: time's up!)

Now look at that list in front of you. Maybe you came up with five things, ten things, or twenty things. Good for you!

Now I want you to take your pen and circle where YOU are on that list.

(Pause.)

Are you even on your own list?

If so, where are you on that list? Are you last or close to it?

Usually when I do this exercise in my workshops, people don't even include themselves on their list. And if they are on their list, they are #8, 9, or 10. This is an aha moment because you realize all of the people, places, and things you are putting ahead of yourself! And this has to change. Why? Because it's the real culprit behind why we are so stressed out, anxious, and overwhelmed.

---

4   Are you really doing this? Fear doesn't want you to, so tell it to hit the road.
     Please play along. It's worth it!

We are so quick to scramble around for everyone else and cancel our plans to make life easier for them that over time, it eats away at us—which leads to us feeling anxiety and resentment. Now, yes, of course we have to cancel plans from time to time. And of course we should do things for others; I'm certainly not saying we shouldn't. Yet when this becomes the norm—all this doing for other people instead of for yourself—you are heading down a dangerous path.

I am officially writing you a permission slip to be selfish! Yes, you! It is 100 percent okay to be selfish, because NOTHING else works unless you are happy, healthy, and taking care of yourself first. Who do you think will benefit the most when you start taking care of yourself with as much effort as you do everyone else? Those closest to you! Your spouse, partner, family, kids. And most of the time, these are the exact people we put ourselves last for time and time again.

I know making yourself a priority is hard, especially for women. We constantly put ourselves last because there are just so many people who need us. However, if you work yourself to death, you could legit end up sick, or worse; then what was the point of it all? All the people who love you and need you no longer have you—and I know that wasn't the reason you worked so hard. Was it?

The only way off this roller coaster of crazy busy is to start, little by little, putting ourselves first. We must make the time, because no one else is ever going to give it to us.

We must make the time, because no one else is ever going to give it to us.

Have you ever woken up and realized you've become someone you don't even recognize? My company sends out these fun VIP forms to our clients after the contract is signed as a way to get to know them so we can celebrate who they are and note special occasions. One of the questions on the form is "What hobbies do you have outside of work?" Someone recently wrote the following (I paraphrase here):

Hobbies? What hobbies? Now that I'm a mom of two kids, there's no time for that. I used to read books, get brunch or mani-pedis with my girlfriends, listen to music in the park, or have dates with my hubby, but that's long gone. Maybe one day again I'll have a life.

This made me so sad—it sounds like she's in jail, rather than living her life, enjoying motherhood, and having fun. I have so many beautiful friends who are mamas, and if I look at those who are the healthiest, happiest, and most balanced, I have to conclude it's the ones who are not afraid to be selfish. They realize that when they go on dates with their husband, brunch with the girls, take bubble baths, get mani-pedis, shop (alone!), and take vacations, they not only have a better relationship with their kids, but they also have a better relationship with their spouse. In taking time for themselves, they are giving their kids an invaluable gift: they model love, happiness, and self-care in motion.

PICK YOURSELF

It's so much easier to sit back and wait than walk into the unknown. The unknown is scary, uncomfy, uncertain, and has no guarantees. So we wait. We wait for all kinds of things: for someone to open the door, for love, for a job, for the promotion, for any way we can be "discovered." Every day there are many opportunities for us to stop waiting and start picking ourselves, yet we miss them because picking yourself is an action that requires courage—and we'd much rather play it safe. We don't want to fail or be embarrassed. Instead, we choose to wait for the right time, the right day, the right boss, the right year, the right amount of "experience." Yet, the problem is when we do this we don't just end up waiting for a really long time, we end up not leveling up at all. And we almost always end up regretting not taking action or advocating for ourselves sooner.

What if instead of fearing failure or the unknown, we started fearing the real bad guy: regret? What if instead of waiting for someone else to decide we're right for a raise or promotion, we decide that we are right for that promotion and start taking action to make that happen?

Seth Godin writes in his blog:

> It's a cultural instinct to wait to get picked. To seek out the permission and authority from [someone] saying "I pick you." Once you reject that impulse and realize that no one is going to select you–that Prince Charming has chosen another house–then you can actually get to work.[5]

No one is coming to save you. You do not need anyone else's permission. You have everything you need already inside you to save your damn self. If you want love, you have to put yourself out there and say how you feel. If you want the promotion, you have to ask for it and then go work your tail off to earn it. If you want to lose weight, you have to show up for yourself and put in the work.

You should always be looking for opportunities to pick, or advocate for, yourself. Equally, you should always be working on your "next job." This is true even if you are an employee of someone else's company or an entrepreneur working a job you created for yourself. You have the ability, even if you don't realize it, to prepare for whatever comes next. And something is always coming. By doing small things every day to make yourself more competitive, you quickly become the one we can't live without.

Think about it: every day you have the stuff you must do and then there's the "other stuff" you seek out: new things to learn, books to read, podcasts to listen to, TED talks to watch, degrees to earn, classes to take, events to attend, boards to join. Picking yourself means adding time into your day so that you can do this "other stuff" as much as (if not more than!!) the work you need to get done.

When you pursue these ways of growing your mind, skillset, and network, you not only stay relevant, but you also become versatile. You will crush boundaries and your value will go up. When you don't look for ways to level up and pick yourself, you end up just staying qualified for the job you have, and you become vulnerable when things change.

A personal example, while I was working full-time in sales and marketing for hotel companies, I was always very involved in our industry associations.

---

5   Seth Godin, "Reject the tyranny of being picked: pick yourself," Seth's Blog, Mar. 21, 2011, https://seths. blog/2011/03/reject-the-tyranny-of-being-picked-pick-yourself.

Even though one was my "job" and the association work I did was unpaid, I looked at them both as equally important to my career success. I would volunteer to join committee after committee, to chair events, and to sit on boards.

When you don't look for ways to level up and pick yourself, you end up just staying qualified for the job you have, and you become vulnerable when things change.

The best part of my volunteer job with the association was that I got to try new things and learn new skills outside my day job without the risk of getting fired. I wrote articles, sat on panels, got better at building content and speaking professionally; I learned how to run a meeting and have tough conversations; and I had the freedom to create new things. When it was time to depart, I believe I left the association a little better than when I joined it.

This kind of skills development is picking yourself. When you are so involved, curious, and open to improvement, you end up becoming even more valuable at your current job. The sales manager who builds a strong brand on social media opens doors to new customers. An HR manager who takes a tech class can end up building a new app for the organization. The VP of marketing who attends a conference brings the ideas back to the organization, lifting up others with these new ideas. All of these people chose to pick themselves. And all of these types of non-paid jobs can make you very valuable.

Let me tell you, throughout my entire career I never once had to search for a job; instead, every opportunity found me. This had everything to do with the fact that I was always looking for opportunities to pick myself rather than waiting for things to come to me, which helped me stay top of mind and valuable. This is why balance matters. You must carve out enough time to do the things that will advance you personally and professionally.

WAYS TO START PICKING YOURSELF

If you are sitting there thinking you have no time for things like this, then I'd say you need to think about how you balance your time and that you probably need to fix your priority list. Whether you are just starting out in business or you are a C-suite running a team, what you do every day to make yourself valuable is a business investment. You must work harder on yourself than you do on your job.

Here are a few easy things you can start doing to pick yourself professionally:

- Volunteer and lead in an industry association.
- Write articles for industry publications.
- Post blogs on LinkedIn.
- Take classes.
- Start watching TED talks.
- Read something every day.
- Raise your hand to lead the next team meeting.
- Submit a session and speak at the next internal or industry conference.
- Cultivate your network continually, not just when you need something.
- Write weekly thank-you notes to people who have helped you, or just surprise someone.
- Take social media classes.
- Attend conferences.
- Hire a coach.

Can you pick one of the ideas on this list and write it into your calendar right now? Can you commit to one that will push you outside your comfort zone and into action?

The questions you should always be asking yourself when you are trying to determine whether you are advocating for yourself enough or if you have achieved balance between your current and future work are these: Am I learning enough? Am I doing enough outside of what I do every day to stay relevant? If push came to shove, am I the one they can't live without?

When you invest in yourself, and your future self, you take the control away from fear and step into your power by building confidence and clarity around who you are and what you are capable of. You open up new doors of possibility because you've realized you have all the tools and permission you'll ever need. You don't need to wait for anyone else to pick you. When you strike a balance between taking care of who you are now while staying focused on where you want to go, YOU become the real boss of your life.

Who's the Boss?

Have you ever accidentally left your phone at home, only to be kind of relieved that you get this random chance to disconnect? Have you ever secretly hoped your plane wouldn't have Wi-Fi so you can't be tempted to log in to email, giving you no other option than to relax, unplug, read, and NOT look at your phone? Have you ever come down with a cold but felt kind of happy to have forced time on the couch to watch endless Netflix shows? Me too, to all the above!

Why does it always seem to take an external force for us to choose to unplug? Why does it take a plane ride or an illness or a forgotten phone for us to wake up to the importance of disconnecting? I once heard productivity guru Michael Hyatt say, "Technology can be an incredible servant but it's a terrible master."

Who's the boss—you, or your technology? Whether you realize it or not, you are running the business of YOU, and a big part of making sure that business is successful is making sure YOU are in control of your time and technology, not the other way around.

The easiest way to feel out of balance and never really get focused is to allow the technology at our fingertips to lure us down a time-wasting path of comparison and distraction. If we want more balance, it's simple: we must put down our phone, take breaks from social media, and stop checking our email every five seconds. Taking time to focus on ourselves is how we achieve true balance.

I know how essential it is to take charge of your time and become a balanced boss. Last year I was traveling on a four-hour direct flight from the East

Coast to the West Coast, and I so needed the white space—the time to disconnect from technology and just be with myself. I wasn't just crazy busy, I was legit going crazy. I didn't want to say no to anything; I wanted to be available for my clients all the time, no matter what. I wanted to do all the things, all the time. I definitely suffer from FOMO (fear of missing out, in case this is a new one for you). I looked forward to getting on this flight because I craved time to disconnect, and I felt ready to finally do just that. No email. No phone. For four whole hours! Just me, my books, my thoughts, my notebook, and the blue sky.

Then, about ten minutes after takeoff, I had my first-ever panic attack. The hot plane probably triggered it, coupled with the fact that I have struggled with an anxiety disorder for more than twenty years. I remember sitting in my seat feeling anxious before the doors even closed, thinking all sorts of things: *Will this plane ever cool down? Why can't I catch my breath? My chest is kinda hurting, am I having a heart attack? Maybe I should get on email to get my mind off it? There is so much to do! What if I miss something? Did I send that contract? I need to update my marketing plan!*

I could not relax. Something bad was happening. My mind was all over the place.

If you've never had a panic attack, here's what they're like: you start to feel like you can't breathe; when you feel like you can't breathe, you think you're going to die; when you think you're going to die, you panic.

It's a spiraling mess. The four hours of zen I was craving turned into one of the scariest days of my life.

You don't want to wait for the rock-bottom moment, the illness, the diagnosis, or the panic attack mid-flight to wake you up to the fact that your life is so pathetically short and you must take care of yourself, now. My panic attack reminded me that while we have to stay connected and get the work done, it's also equally important to take a deep breath and have the courage to disconnect. To remind your brain that YOU are okay, you are safe, and you are the boss—not the panic. My brain panicked because I was exhausted and overwhelmed, yes; but it also panicked because I wasn't doing the work on myself to mentally handle all the moving pieces. That sort of neglect is not sustainable. You have to boss up for yourself and make a choice about how you run your day, every day.

That day on the plane taught me an important lesson. There will be times in life that you literally can't leave an uncomfortable situation, so you have to buckle up and hold on. I was ten minutes into a four-hour flight. There was no getting off that plane, so it became me vs. myself. And I decided that I was not going to lose. So, I started calming myself down by taking action: I asked the stranger next to me to talk to me and keep me calm; I did as much deep breathing as I could; I asked the flight attendant to borrow her fun magazines to keep my mind distracted; and she kept the cups of ice flowing for me (ice is your BFF in a panic attack because heat is a trigger). Then, as soon as we landed, I went to a doctor and got medical treatment and also made sure there wasn't something even worse happening.

These days, my mind and I have a different relationship. I no longer take for granted the feeling of peace, and I work hard to keep my mental health in check, which includes a good amount of disconnecting from the world so I can reconnect with myself.

My brain panicked because I was exhausted and overwhelmed, yes; but it also panicked because I wasn't doing the work on myself to mentally handle all the moving pieces.

You are the boss, not your iPhone, not your email, not your social media. Whether you work for yourself or someone else, you always have a choice. You find yourself craving time to unplug, because in order to keep the lights on in the business of you, your body literally needs to have time to recharge. Without rest, you can't be the best version of yourself and you most certainly won't stay in business, or be any fun to work with, if you are sick and exhausted all the time.

A Quick Rant about Email

Think about your day-to-day actions—specifically your morning routine. What do you do when you wake up? Are you spending the first few hours taking care of you? Or are you immediately jumping right into your email and hustling for everyone else's to-do lists? It's highly likely you are even sleeping with your phone by your bed, that you are checking email before bed, before you even drink your coffee in the morning. This madness has to stop!

Here are some crazy stats for you:

- Workers with an iPhone spend about 70 percent of their day engaging with it.[6]
- 6.3 hours a day are spent on email.[7]
- 55 percent of workers check email after 11 p.m.[8]
- 81 percent of workers check their work email on weekends.[9]
- 59 percent of workers keep on top of their work email while on vacation.[10]

This one takes my breath away: 6.3 hours a day are spent on email. And we wonder why we can't get anything done. Just imagine how much you could change your life, and the world, if you cut that number in half. So, fear BOSS, are you running your life and your schedule, or are you letting your email boss you around?

The moment you realize that email is simply everyone else's to-do lists, you shift your perspective on the rush of it all. Your #1 goal should be to tend to your priorities first, then respond to the rest of the world.

A few ideas to get you thinking that can really change the game on how you look at and handle your email:

1. Use the three Ds of email to keep a zero inbox. Either do it, delete it, or delegate it. Period.

2. Each morning ask yourself, What is the "one thing" I can do first today that will make the rest of my day easier, better, and/or more productive? Then go do it.

---

6 See https://www.ccl.org/wp-content/uploads/2015/04/AlwaysOn.pdf.
7 See Adobe Software Study, https://www.huffingtonpost.com/entry/check-work-email-hours-survey _us_55ddd168e4b0a40aa3ace672.
8 See GFI software study, https://www.prnewswire.com/news-releases/survey-checking-email-at-night-on-weekends-and-holidays-is-the-new-norm-for-us-workforce-207352741.html.
9 Ibid.
10 Ibid.

3. Do not check email first thing. Take the first few hours of your day to work on your "one thing" first. *(More on how to structure your schedule coming up!)*

4. Every Sunday, sit down and plan out your week. Then, each night before bed, look at the next day to make sure things make sense, and pivot where necessary. Always be looking for white space. Are you leaving a buffer?

5. Remove distractions. When you are working on a task, are you focused? We think that decluttering is a waste of time, but research shows that when we remove clutter and distractions, we can increase productivity by 50 percent. Yes, this means a clean, clutter-free desk is a productive one!

6. Read the books *Essentialism: The Disciplined Pursuit of Less* (by Greg McKeown) and *The One Thing: The Surprisingly Simple Truth Behind Extraordinary Results* (Gary Keller and Jay Papasan). Absolute game changers.

You have the power to change your life by simply making a few brave choices on how you run your day. If you can't remember the last time you got everything done on your to-do list with time to spare, these ideas will help you get back in the slay saddle.

Regulators Mount Up

When you hit the pause button on human beings, rather than pausing, we actually *start*. This is why some of us get our best ideas in the shower or while on vacation. (Remember: I came up with the idea for *Fear Is My Homeboy* while on my honeymoon with my husband!) The moment you slow down, your entire body gets recharged. Think of your iPhone . . . the battery wears down when you use it too much. So what do you do? You plug it into the wall so you can recharge it. And honestly, we are kinder to our iPhones than we are ourselves. Well, why don't we let ourselves recharge? Why don't we worry about our battery running out? Don't we realize that we can, and do, run out of juice just like a cell phone? We have got to learn to regulate.

Recent studies show that those who give in to some kind of break or distraction once per hour perform better than those who just keep at it without a break. After a while, our brains become numb to the constant stimulation and we start to look at the task as unimportant. When you take a break, you can come back to your task at hand with fresh energy and a renewed sense of purpose.[11] This science-backed "one break per hour" idea is a regulator moment. This is you plugging in your iPhone.

Being a regulator means you check yourself before you wreck yourself, you slow down on purpose, you step back and observe, you take breaks, take naps, think before you say yes, go on vacations, play hooky once in a while, and stop worrying so much about what everyone else is saying and/or doing. Regulating, even if it seems like it's taking time away from you, actually ends up expanding your time because you start to get a healthy perspective on what really matters in the long run.

I get it. This all sounds great, and right now you are probably thinking, "I have zero time to regulate; there is no way I can make that happen." Again, fear. Excuses are fear. You do have the time, and you can become a regulator if you make this a priority. Whatever you focus on expands. Period. When you choose to pick yourself, you have to regulate: it's a job requirement. This means slowing your roll, hitting that pause button, and doing things that advance YOU as much as you do things to advance everyone else. Yes, you read that right . . . you must work harder on yourself than you do on your job.

Whatever you focus on expands. Period.

REGULATE YOUR SCHEDULE

Whether you run your own business or work for someone else, you have got to take charge of your schedule so that you can build balance into your days. Remember: what you focus on expands! You want to make more sales, focus on

---

11   *Science News*, "Brief diversions vastly improve focus, researchers find," Feb. 8, 2011, www.sciencedaily.com.

it. You want to lose weight, focus on it. You want to earn a degree, focus on it. You want to get a raise, focus on it.

To inspire you a little bit, I've shared my schedule here to give you a sneak peek into how I regulate before taking care of the rest of the world:

	Monday	Tuesday	Wednesday	Thursday	Friday
Mornings (7a.m.-11a.m.)	Creating TED talks	Rehearsals Research	Think Mediate Move Body	Get Outside Reading	Freestyle Fridays!
Afternoons (1p.m.-5p.m.)	Email Phone Calls	Meetings Follow Up 20 min Nap	Accounting Errands	Gifts Packing	Freestyle Fridays!

Let's break down how my schedule works to encourage balance so I get more freedom.

As you read this, keep in mind that this schedule is how I roll 90 percent of the time. There are days and weeks where I get off balance because I'm on the road for a super-long stretch or I go on vacation, but I try to keep this focused-hustle structure non-negotiable.

I'd also like to point out that the bullet points listed in each a.m./p.m. section are not things I do every day; they are simply the pool of tasks I typically make priorities in each part of my day. Personally, my mornings are when I'm the most energized. Plus, I find I'm more successful when I take care of myself and all my creative projects first, before I get distracted by my email or my workday. Thus, the mornings are my structured time to focus on all the creative things I do in my business and for myself. Then, in my afternoons, when I'm usually burning out anyway, I can focus on the more tactical aspects of my business, like taking phone calls, responding to email, and sitting in meetings.

Third, notice I leave buffer time . . . in the middle of the day Monday through Thursday, and all day on Friday, which I call my Freestyle Fridays. This doesn't mean I don't work on Friday, it means I freestyle: I leave it open to flexibility in case something happens in the week or pops up that gets me off track.

This buffer is a massive schedule hack that allows me to not freak out when life doesn't go my way. Example: You get the flu bug on Tuesday, so you miss work; not a worry, you can use Friday to catch up!

Last, I always force myself to get OUT of the office at lunchtime. Most of us eat our lunch at our desks, rarely leaving the building. I challenge you to get out into nature, go eat with a colleague, take a walk, move your body. You must mix up your workday.

I know a senior executive who works in downtown Chicago. After I shared my schedule ideas with her, she started to do something similar. She leads a team of five and has a very demanding job with lots of moving parts. She decided to read the book *Essentialism* and share the ideas with her leadership to get their buy-in. Her goal: to run an experiment with her schedule to see how it would affect her personally and professionally if she started structuring her day differently.

So she decided to mix it up, and here's how she spends her workweek now. From 8:30 to 11:30 each morning, she works on HER business. She puts a fun "do not disturb" sign on her door, she takes no meetings, does not answer phone calls, and does not look at email. Then at 11:30 she opens her door, goes to lunch, and returns around 1:00 p.m. From 1:00 p.m. to 5:00 p.m. her door is open; she sits in meetings, takes calls, responds to email, and does the tactical stuff that needs to get done.

This is how she rolls 90 percent of the time now. Of course she has to be flexible, but that's not difficult now that her working schedule has a buffer in it. Because of this new way of working, she is reaping rewards personally and professionally! This is what she's accomplished in one year:

- Lost twenty-five pounds
- Earned TWO advanced industry degrees
- Increased sponsor revenues for her annual conference by 35 percent
- Got a promotion that came with a nice salary increase
- Read fifteen books
- Reduced staff turnover by almost 100 percent

You'll notice that both my friend and I save our tactical tasks for the afternoon, while we leave the mornings focused on us. We both do things each morning—BEFORE we check email—that will advance our personal and professional goals. This gives us both the gift of freedom, because we are designing our schedules to be more focused, more flexible, and more FUN!

Another client of mine, who is a director of HR, actually sends her entire team an Outlook appointment making it "mandatory" they take one hour of self-care each day.

One hour a day can make a massive difference. That's 5 hours a week, 20 hours a month, or 240 hours a year. Just imagine how much this amount of personal development could change your life!

Tips for Convincing Your Employer to Regulate Your Schedule

Of course, if you are not the "boss," you want to get your leadership involved so there is buy-in from the top down before you start making changes like this.

Here are a few ideas to help you "sell it" to your leadership:

· Focus on the results.

If you do x, y, or z, here is how we will build new revenue streams, increase performance, and/or reduce turnover. Make it about what you will do for "them" and the organization so they see that you have plans to level up on all fronts.

· Find a way to make it their idea.

Do they follow anyone or really respect a certain leader/author? Maybe there is a book you can pass along or an example you can share from someone who did something similar and changed the game.

· Start small.

Even one hour a day can be a game changer.

· Use data.

Most CFOs and CEOs like the bottom line because they are responsible for it. Share research and data showing how this new schedule can increase performance.

You, FearBoss, are not a damn robot. You are a human being, not a human doing. Your body needs rest and love and sweat and self-care as much as you need food and water. It's time to stop feeling so ashamed of wanting this, and time to start going out and getting it.

How to Make Fear Your Homeboy
AND BECOME A MORE BALANCED #FEARBOSS:

1. Rethink the way you incentivize your team.

The traditional ways of incentivizing employees have changed. Everyone has a different vibe, different goals, and different priorities. Have you evaluated how employees really want to be incentivized? Offer the following perks in conjunction with, or instead of, the traditional bonus check:

- A flexible schedule, where the employee can work from home one to three days a week for a certain amount of time.
- Give them a certain number of "paid" days off with no blackout dates.
- Offer the ability to work from a private office (introverts) or a cool coworking space (extroverts) to inspire creativity and more focus.
- Pay for them to earn an advanced degree, a certification, or take a business-related class.
- Pay for them to attend any business conference they want to expand their network and enhance their skills.

2. Design a schedule that gives you freedom.

Most of us use our calendars incorrectly. We don't schedule real work, we schedule "interruptions." Meetings, doctor visits, phone calls. All distractions and, in most cases, other people's work. As Eric Barker writes in his book, *Barking Up the Wrong Tree*: "If real work is the stuff that affects the bottom line, the stuff that gets you noticed, the thing that earns you raises and gets you singled out for promotion, well, let me utter blasphemy and suggest that maybe it deserves a little dedicated time too."[12]

Use the template below to start thinking about restructuring your day so that your real work happens before all the interruptions. Can you take the first 60, 90, or 120 minutes of your day to advance your professional and personal goals first? Before you check your email. Are you more focused in the morning, or do you do your best work in the afternoon? Can you get your leadership on board? How will restructuring your day impact the bottom line for you personally, and at work?

	Monday	Tuesday	Wednesday	Thursday	Friday
Mornings (7a.m.-11a.m.)					
Afternoons (1p.m.-5p.m.)					

3. Take a nappuccino.

There is a large body of research suggesting that naps improve cognitive performance and boost mental and physical health. If you want to make a real contribution to the world, the best asset you have is you. Yet we constantly underinvest in ourselves—in the most common way, by skipping sleep. Greg McKeown writes in the game-changing productivity book *Essentialism*: "If you think you are so tough you can do anything I have a challenge for you. If you really want to do something hard: say no to an opportunity so you can take a nap."

---

12   *Barking Up the Wrong Tree: The Surprising Science Behind Why Everything You Know About Success Is (Mostly) Wrong* (New York: HarperOne, 2017), 253.

Yes, please! Naps don't need to be long to be effective. That's why the nap-puccino is brilliant! According to Daniel Pink,[13] it works like this:

· Find your afternoon low point. This is usually about seven hours after you've woken up.

· Create a peaceful environment for your nap. Did you know that companies are now installing nap rooms into their offices and conferences are incorporating nap teepees for participants to recharge?

· Down a cup of coffee. This makes it the nappuccino, and the caffeine will take about twenty-five minutes to hit your bloodstream.

· Set a timer for twenty-five minutes. It may take you five minutes to doze off, and naps between ten and twenty minutes are the sweet spot, measurably boosting energy right when that caffeine is about to kick in!

· Repeat. Nappers that nap a lot get more from their naps than those who don't. So it's time to get your nap on!

4. Drop everything and learn.

I mentioned how I have a client who sends a calendar appointment to her team putting mandatory self-care time on their work calendars. This is something you could implement as a leader to help foster an environment of self-care and balance.

Use the following email as inspiration for when you communicate the task of scheduling self-care time to your employees:

To: (your team)
Subject: DEAL—Drop Everything and Learn
Location: A meeting room, your car, outside, or wherever you
          are at this time
Time: Daily from 1:00 to 2:00 p.m.

---

13   Daniel Pink, "Nappuccino: A Scientific 5-Step Guide to the Perfect Nap," 2018, www.danpink.com.

Team,

As you know, I continue to fight the good fight for self-care and personal development. It's far too easy to get caught up in taking care of everyone else that we forget ourselves. (guilty as charged)

DEAL stands for Drop Everything and Learn. You owe yourself sixty minutes of "you" time. Here are some ideas for how to use this block of time each day:

- Listen to a podcast
- Watch a TED Talk
- Read a business book
- Take an online course
- Reflect on your own personal brand and take time to think about your superpowers and how you define you

5. Read something every day.

A great way to stay relevant is to make a lifelong commitment to continual personal development. There is research that shows if you read just ten minutes per day (which typically equals ten pages per day for the average reader), in one year's time you will have read nineteen 200-page books. Just imagine how much your life will change when you are reading nineteen 200-page life, business, and personal development books! It's hard to get stuck somewhere old when you are always learning something new.

Don't forget to share your #FearIsMyHomeboy moments on social! Tag me and use the hashtag when you make any of these boss moves. I want to celebrate with you!

CHAPTER 4

Becoming the CEO of You

"It's not about what you've got.
It's about how brave you're prepared to be."
—SETH GODIN

Now that you are a balanced #FearBoss, it's time to spend a little time focusing on the "boss" part of things. If you want to manage your fear, you must stop thinking of yourself only as an employee who works for someone else and start thinking of yourself as a CEO. That's right. A badass, C-suite, world-dominating CEO! Whether you run your own biz or work for a company, you are the chief energy officer in the business of YOU before anything else! By identifying, protecting, and establishing your personal brand, you can start to differentiate yourself in the marketplace, and your industry, by delivering on promises, building trust, and thinking of yourself as a business with powerful assets that must be protected at all costs.

You Are a Business

Yes, you are working *in* business, but you are also running *a* business: the business of you. You are a walking, talking, living, breathing business—and you are the CEO. Your personal brand, your mental health, your physical health, your stamina, and your habits are just a few of the critical pieces in managing the C-suite of you.

When you think of yourself as an actual business, you shift your perspective from "I collect a paycheck" to "I am on a mission." A mission not only to earn money to pay your bills, but a mission to stay healthy so you can do that, a mission to inspire others, a mission to leave things better than you found them, a mission to do work that matters, and a mission to hustle for joy over stress. A badass CEO Fear Boss doesn't do basic. Basic is still in bed. You are awake and ready. Ready to do the work required to protect your assets.

This is the approach that I take in my own life: I run my company HOLLA! Productions, and I also operate the business of Judi Holler, the person. There would be no HOLLA! Productions without a happy, healthy Judi Holler, so I work harder on Judi Holler than you'd expect. Judi Holler "the business" invests in people to help her; she hires people smarter than she is; she has mentors who are fifty and mentors who are twenty. She doesn't skip doctor visits, rides hard on the Peloton bike, reads every day, has a biz coach, goes to seminars, takes online courses, gets massages, uses her vacation days, and doesn't let email boss her around. Judi the biz is a well-oiled machine, and she doesn't let fear make her feel guilty about being selfish for protecting her biz assets, no matter what!

Okay, this writing in third person is starting to get weird, but hopefully you are catching my vibe here. You are a business. That business has powerful assets. You must protect them. Doing this is your algorithm to long-term stamina and stability, both personally and professionally.

Work Your Assets Off

As the chief energy officer of yourself, you have to protect the assets inside your organization. Just like the president or CEO of an actual company or association has to protect the assets inside that organization, including the employees and stable finances, you have to do the same thing as the CEO of your company. There is no one looking out for you but you. If you want to stay relevant in business, it's critical you are alert to this idea because your assets are what will keep you employed, healthy, and thriving.

Those assets are things such as your—

- **Energy.** Your energy is mental. It's your physical and emotional well-being. Are you mentally, physically, and emotionally prepared for the highs and lows of life?

- **Intellectual property.** Your IP is your brain capital. It's your base of knowledge. How much do you know and are you learning enough?

- **Habits.** Your habits are actions. They're the things you do daily, weekly, and monthly that advance your life and create the actual change. Have you developed any rituals or routines that put into motion your actual goals?

- **Strategic focus.** Your strategic focus is the roadmap. It's your ability to see the big picture while still taking action on what matters today. Do you have tools in your life to help you stay in forward momentum?

As the chief energy officer of yourself, you have to protect the assets inside your organization.

Now that you realize what your most powerful biz assets are, you have to think about what you are doing to protect each one of them. The first things that seem to get cut when you're stressed out, overwhelmed, and exhausted are these very assets. We think, "Who has the time?" or "I'll get to it," or "Once I get less busy, I'll figure it out." Spoiler alert: less busy is not coming. You will never *not* be "busy." You must start putting plans in place now to protect each of the assets above in order to build a business that lasts.

When you cut things like vacations, sleep, time with friends/family, fitness, and eating right to get "caught up at work or at home," you stay stuck, safe, and just the same. Fear *loves* this. This is how fear makes you sick and miserable. Maybe you have a big presentation to give, but instead of putting blocks of time into your calendar to prepare, you wait until the last minute and end up canceling plans with friends or working late to catch up. Maybe you have the kids to yourself all week due to a traveling spouse, but instead of planning meals ahead of time, you end up ghosting the gym and hitting the drive-thru most nights because you are overwhelmed. Maybe you run a business, but because you can't "let go" or delegate to your team, you live on the road and never see your family. These are all examples of fear-negative approaches.

When fear gets in your way and causes you to make choices that are easy and unhealthy versus choices that require courage in order for you to protect you and your time, you're letting fear control your life in a negative way. A fear-positive approach is when you use fear to motivate you into positive action and preparation. This is you knowing a scary situation is coming up, so instead of not thinking about it, you "boss up" for yourself and put plans in place to prepare for it. You must protect your assets at all costs.

> **Energy:** Protecting your mental, physical, and emotional well-being
>
> **Intellectual Property:** Protecting your brain power
>
> **Habits:** Protecting your routines
>
> **Strategic Focus:** Protecting your time

Life is going to get crazy, and things will get off balance from time to time because there is always a trade-off. Yet, when you are protecting your assets, it's much easier to handle any disruption that comes your way because fear is not the boss—you are.

WEIGHING TRADE-OFFS

Society tells us, incorrectly, that we can have it all. Messages about how we must do everything or have everything are woven into advertising, marketing, and social media, making us think something must be wrong with us if we don't "have it all." Here's the thing—we *can't* have it all. It's literally not possible. There is always a trade-off on the other side of any choice you make. Always.

Even if you set badass goals with realistic expectations, what makes the goals realistic is realizing there is a trade-off. Saying yes to an opportunity almost always requires you to say no to several others. Additionally, when you say yes to a job, a role, or a career path, you ultimately are also saying yes to the trade-offs that come with the role. If you've negotiated that trade-off with yourself early on, you can manage your expectations on the back end. Following are some examples.

You are:	The trade-off:
A keynote speaker.	Living in airports and no sick days.
An author.	Hard deadlines and nasty reviews.
A parent.	Lack of sleep and financial stress.
Leading a team.	More pressure and having a team to care for.
An actor.	Unstable pay and no guarantee of work.

All of the above choices and roles have good stuff that *far* outweighs the trade-offs, but still there are opportunity costs to growing into new roles. Look at Oprah, for example; most would agree she "has it all." She is worth millions, has estates in the most magical places, flies on private jets, has built an empire that inspires millions daily, and does work that is changing the world. Yet, I wonder. Does she really have "it all"? There are no doubt trade-offs she's made along the way: she is not married, does not have kids, lives in the public eye, gets sued, and has had plenty of people publicly bash her. Of course the good FAR exceeds the bad, yet she still deals with trade-offs.

As the CEO of you, understanding that trade-offs are real will help you get focused and end up saving you trouble. When you haven't weighed all the trade-offs for any choice you want to make or for any role you are about to take on, then you risk the possibility of being miserable, burning out, not doing a good job, and wasting a ton of time. When you get crystal clear on the good, bad, and ugly of any choice you are about to make, you can get yourself mentally prepared for what may happen. Reasonable trade-offs do not put you in dangerous situations; they encourage change, help you evolve, open new doors, and push you outside your comfort zone. Unreasonable trade-offs hurt others, hurt you, don't align with your core values, and are usually things you do for someone else.

The best book I've ever read on balance and productivity, which I've mentioned earlier, is *Essentialism* by Greg McKeown. He writes, "Trade-offs are real, in our personal and professional lives. We can try to avoid the reality of trade-offs, but we can't escape them."[14]

You may think that somehow you'll be able to juggle it all, make it all work, or have it all. Yet, this sort of thinking is not realistic or sustainable. When you can check yourself before you wreck yourself, which means getting clear on what the trade-offs are FIRST, you set yourself up for success and can save so much disappointment on the back end. One of my favorite things to do before I take on any new project or job and before making any big choice or decision is to "T-square it up." This means I put the job, project, choice, or decision at the top of a blank piece of paper and then I draw two columns. Column #1 says Good/Amazing, and Column #2 says Bad/Ugly. Then I jam out on it thinking of all the things that could come up in each column. After I've spent at least thirty minutes doing this, I visually take a look at which column is longer, and that gives me a nice snapshot of where I should be leaning and gets me looking at the trade-offs from the start.

Good/Amazing   Bad/Ugly

---

14 *Essentialism: The Disciplined Pursuit of Less* (New York: Currency, 2014), 54.

Mark Manson calls trade-offs "sh*t sandwiches" in *The Subtle Art of Not Giving a F*ck*. He also knows that every single thing you say yes to has a trade-off. He writes in his blog, "Everything sucks, some of the time. If you want to be a professional artist, but you aren't willing to see your work rejected hundreds, if not thousands of times, then you're done before you start."[15]

You have to decide what flavor of sh*t sandwich you are willing to eat. Only you can decide what level of suckage you will tolerate. As Manson writes in his blog, "Everything involves sacrifice. Everything includes some sort of cost. Nothing is pleasurable or uplifting all of the time. So the question becomes: what struggle or sacrifice are you willing to tolerate?"[16]

Once you've weighed the trade-offs, you can feel better about the focus you have on achieving a specific goal. This focus, this asset that you protect as CEO of you, comes from balancing the risks and rewards and deciding what's best for you.

Bring a Brick

In improv theater, we are taught to bring a brick. The brick has a specific meaning: focus on what you can contribute and just bring one thing into the scene at a time. It's easy to get caught up in the excitement happening onstage in a live improv show, to want to build an improv house right away and dump everything you've got onto the stage. We see how amazing and fun and badass this house will be, so we grab whatever we think could be useful for reaching this goal and just show up with a bucketload of bricks, dumping them onto the stage floor and expecting our castmates to "figure it out." *Can't they see the house that I see? Why can't they make sense of the bricks I just brought?*

This is a signature move of most early improvisers. Instead of focusing on the next thing, we try to bring the best things and everything, which means we bring way too much in hopes something will stick. This is a bad move because it immediately clutters the stage (and scene) with way too much information. It also means that the other improvisers don't know where to start or where to go next, because there is just too much going on. Bringing a bucket of bricks is

---

15   Mark Manson, "7 Strange Questions that Help You Find Your Life Purpose," MM.net, https://markmanson.net/life-purpose.
16   Ibid.

a fear-based action because you don't feel that the one brick you have is good enough, so you bring them all to the party in order to protect yourself from having nothing to contribute. When really, if you'd just trust yourself (and of course trust the other players), you'd find that you already have everything you need inside you. Less is always more on an improv stage.

We don't want your bucket of bricks; all we need is just one brick. Then let's have some fun and build the foundation of the house together. You don't need to build the entire house all by yourself. When you're working and collaborating with others, it's exhausting and not nearly as fun as when you try to do all the work yourself. Plus, you immediately isolate others from you because you cut them out of the process of building or creating or doing whatever it is that you are working on as a team. And the process is the gift. Trust that there is power in the collective group's brainpower, and do not allow fear to make you doubt your unique contribution.

There is a classic improv exercise that helps with the concept of slowing down and focusing on one thing at a time. It's called "one word." This game is easy to play and teaches the lesson of only bringing one brick at a time and trusting that the brick you bring is exactly what is needed. This game is designed to help you think on your feet and be flexible, yet it's mostly designed to teach you the power of just bringing one small contribution to a project. Your group will end up creating a super-funny and organic story all while demonstrating listening, teamwork, and the power of bringing one brick.

Here's how it works:

· Grab a group of three to ten people and sit in a circle.

· The group will tell a shared story, each person contributing one word at a time.

· Get a suggestion from the audience if you have one, or pull an idea out of a bowl, like "what is something work colleagues normally talk about?" Then let that inspire your story.

· You start with one person, pick a leader, to say the first word, then you'll go around the circle telling this made-up story one word at a time.

- You can use punctuation like a period, question mark, or exclamation point as a word to make a point or add context/humor.
- After a few minutes, end the exercise and talk about it.

How did it feel to use only one word? What was it like to think on your feet? How did it feel to not know what was coming next? What was it like having to trust the group and the process?

You have everything it takes to be successful. When you slow down and focus on the one next thing, and stop worrying about having the best thing, you will get way more focused. This "strategic focus" is a massive asset for the business of who you are.

FOCUS, YO!

You have a million tasks to complete every day: phone calls, meetings, email, kid stuff, errands, social events, business travel, exercising . . . oh, and not to mention feeding yourself and drinking a glass of red to wind down. When was the last time you got everything done on your to-do list with time to spare? Even if you don't believe it, you DO have the time. You just need a roadmap for developing your ability to strategically focus. This asset is a game changer.

I define "strategic focus" as having your eye on the big picture of tomorrow yet staying connected, and taking action, on what matters today. Here's the deal. You have so much you want to do every day, yet we never really get any of it done. Why? Because we are hustling the wrong way.

When you can find a way to focus on one thing at a time, bringing just a brick each day to advance your goals, you start making progress. And the badass side effect is that all of a sudden you start getting stuff done and begin crossing things off your list, which leads to motivation. Once you get motivated, you invite momentum to the party—and momentum is an unstoppable force of "HELL YES!" that can withstand more than you think, including jealousy, comparison, and self-doubt.

IF SOMEONE ELSE CAN HAVE IT, SO CAN YOU!

If you want to immediately give up on all of your goals and never get strategically focused, spend your time being jealous. Comparison is deadly, especially as the CEO of you, because you must understand that NO ONE does it your way. No one has your specific set of gifts, talents, and ideas, so you cannot measure your success by comparing it to the success of others.

You've had these moments when you are scrolling through social media and all you wanted was to respond to the new comments on your last post or see your BFF's latest trip pictures, but then all of a sudden it's an hour later and you're falling down a self-comparison social media black hole, ending up on your coworker's ex-boyfriend's cousin's page, wondering how the hell you got there. You begin looking at person after person, page after page, comparing your life with what you're seeing others have or do. What started out as an innocent stroll through social, ends up making you want to rethink everything you're doing—and you fill with self-doubt.

In *Girl Code: Unlocking the Secrets to Success, Sanity, and Happiness for the Female Entrepreneur*, author Cara Alwill Leyba writes about a study in the *Journal of Science* that says, "the feeling of jealousy actually activates a region of the brain involved in processing physical pain." Well, damn. No wonder jealousy hurts! The good news here is that feeling jealous of someone else isn't all bad, because in most cases it's holding up a mirror to what you want more of for yourself in your own life. It means you want to level up, so fear comes in—hot with jealousy to stop you from taking action.

Comparison and jealousy are two of fear's BFFs because if there is one quick way for fear to get you to quit or to lose focus, this is it. Fear wants you to think you aren't ready, that you aren't good enough, or that it's already all been done before. This could not be further from the truth. You are one of a kind. You are irreplaceable. And you are an original. Having the courage to be authentically, and unapologetically, who you are is a powerful Fear BOSS tool, because no one else can be you.

Remember these two things when you are facing comparison and jealousy:

1. Blinders are everything—focus on your own race.

Have you ever watched a horse race? If not, spoiler alert! They put blinders on those badass beauties. Why? So they can't look left or right because if they do, they risk falling or tripping, and in a high-speed horse race this small mistake can be fatal. This is why horses wear blinders—so they can't look at what's going on around them in order to stay safe and run their own race. How can you let this idea inspire you to channel your inner Kentucky Derby goddess the next time you are tempted to waste your energy worrying about, and obsessing over, what everyone else is doing? When you are busy being the CEO of your business, you have no time for petty distractions because you know that comparison is fear's way of getting you to trip up and lose focus.

2. Stop hating and start studying.

I recently heard Franchesca Ramsey interviewed by Marie Forleo on an episode of *Marie TV*, and she said something that made me change my entire perspective on jealousy. Franchesca said, "Stop hating and start studying." This #micdrop moment means you must stop spending so much time feeling jealous and spend more time being inspired by others so you can start taking action on the things you want to get done for yourself. If there is someone you are starting to envy or feel competitive with, become a student and look for opportunities to learn from them rather than wasting time looking for all the things wrong with them. There is power in saying: "Damn, she really *is* amazing! She really *is* killing it! Well, if she can do it, maybe so can I!" Turn your negative self-talk into positive actions that will advance your goals inch by inch, day by day. As the CEO of you, you don't have time for jealousy because you realize that:

fear competes and confidence empowers!

A real Fear BOSS takes their envy and turns it into fuel for their own fire. You must let those who are out there blazing trails inspire you to focus on blazing a trail of your own! When you feel jealous or competitive, remember this:

there is likely someone less talented and less amazing than you who has already done the thing you wish to do. If they can do it, so can you! Spend your time getting strategically focused and understanding what your passions are.

What Are Your Passion Patterns?

It's really hard to get focused when you have zero clue what you want to do, where you want to go, and what lights you up. Every decade, you will be a different version of you. Which means your personal brand, and passions, will evolve over time. What you like, what you do, and who you are will change because YOU are changing. This is okay, totally normal, and actually amazing, so lean into it.

Here's an experiment I learned from a friend that might help you if you feel lost, unfocused, and can't seem to find your passion right now: for thirty days, keep a notebook by your bed, and every night before bed answer this question: What was my favorite thing I did today?

Now, of course your kids and spouse and friends will always be your favorites . . . but try to push yourself and move outside the family. Try keeping a personal list and a professional list. After thirty days, what do you notice? You should start to pick up on patterns that could spark inspiration and give you some direction if you are feeling unhappy and unfocused. It's hard to set goals and do the work when we don't know what it is that lights us up or what it is that we really want for ourselves. Once you have that clarity, you can start to put a plan in place. And fear hates plans. Because plans mean action and action means change; yet what stops us is the fact that change feels scary. The antidote: having a focused yet strategic roadmap. Which means keeping your eye on the big picture of tomorrow while taking action on what matters today. This is another important superpower in the biz you're running as CEO of you.

ROCK A 30-DAY YEAR

I practice this focused-hustle approach and call it my "30 Rock." About 90 percent of my life and business is managed in 30-day windows. This means taking your big goals and breaking them down into actionable steps in shorter time frames. Think about any runner who's ever crossed a finish line. It all began when they signed up for the race. Then they ran the first mile. Then the next. And so on. Before you know it, you've crossed the finish line and done the unthinkable.

We don't need you to do it all right now, we just need you to start with the first step. When you bring things into smaller windows, you invite focus to the party and fear can't stand up to focus. Now, this doesn't mean you aren't thinking about the big picture. You are—big time. But what matters the most is what are you doing today, this week, and this month to make your dreams, goals, and desires a reality. What action are you taking right now? Dreams without deadlines are just fairytales; and as much as I love myself a Disney princess, I much prefer results. Deadlines give you results.

Dreams without deadlines are just fairytales.

When you work in smaller segments—30 Rocks—you not only get laser focused, but you also get more confident. You start to make progress, you start to cross things off your list, you get momentum . . . all this brings fuel to the focus fire. Plus, working in 30-day windows gives you twelve New Year's Eves to check in with yourself, make any changes, pivot where necessary, and my favorite—to celebrate your success! Having a roadmap in place to help you focus on your goals will ensure you make the waves needed to advance yourself.

Make Waves

It's easy to do things the same way we've always done them, to wait, hide, and make yourself smaller. Why? Because it's scary to make waves, or try something new and put yourself out there, because it means you will get noticed or have to level up. While riding waves may seem fun and easy at first, real change happens when you MAKE your own waves. This means getting outside of your comfort zone and doing things that will challenge you. If you want career stability, a raise, or that promotion, you must do things to stay top of mind. If you want love, better health, or more balance in your life, you have to do things that put those goals in motion. I get that for some of us it can feel scary to be seen, and others of us don't want to be seen at all. You must realize this is fear trying to make you doubt yourself. You don't need to speak on a stage or be loud to get noticed. Making waves is all about making strategic moves that keep you top of mind with clients, prospects, and your leadership, all while staying in motion toward your goals.

Are you challenging yourself enough personally and professionally, or are you going through the motions? When was the last time you got a raise or a promotion? How long have you been at your company and in your role? Are you staying because you love it or because it's "safe"? Are you riding waves or making them?

We need you to make waves. We want you to cause a ruckus. Be unexpected. Think about how you can make waves and incorporate new, positive changes with your team, your clients, and your leadership. These changes don't have to be huge to have a large impact. This might be how you think about things as someone who "rides the wave":

> Today we will make sales calls—better grab bagels at Panera.
>
> Today we will have our all-team meeting—better polish that PowerPoint presentation.
>
> Today we will give employee reviews—better print the HR forms for everyone to sign.
>
> Today we will host a client event—better book a banquet room.

Why not do the unexpected and make some waves? It's way more fun to blow minds. Here's an edited version of the above to give you an example of what these small changes could be:

> Today we will make sales calls—let's bring cake pops and confetti.
>
> Today we will have our all-team meeting—let's rent a karaoke machine.

Today we will give employee reviews—let's give everyone a free day off with pay.

Today we will host a client event—let's do the meeting in the park with hot dogs and snow cones!

You don't have to be übercreative or a mad scientist to make waves. Anyone can make a wave. All it takes is a little effort each week spending time thinking about your processes and challenging yourself to think OUTSIDE the box. And you can try incorporating fun changes to make waves both personally and professionally. At work, ask yourself: When was the last time we looked at this process? Is there something we aren't seeing? How can it improve? Are we doing things the same way we've always done them because no one's suggested doing them differently?

You can also ask yourself questions like: How can I surprise and delight my spouse, boss, or friends today? How can I do the opposite of what everyone expects at work or at home? What can I do to exceed expectations with my clients or family this week?

Start small. Even a tiny ripple in the water is still motion. That's what this is all about. Staying in forward momentum and inviting yourself to the party, rather than waiting for an invitation. Making waves is an incredible way to stop hiding and start differentiating your brand and establishing the business of you.

Shame Is Lame

When did it become a bad thing to express joy and pride and confidence about what you do for a living? It can be uncomfortable to toot your own horn about your accomplishments and desires because we don't want to come off like we have a big ego. Figuring out *how* to put yourself out there in a way that builds trust, provides value, and makes you look like a badass (and not a brag) is a huge part of being the CEO of you.

The world tells us to feel ashamed when we talk about ourselves because it's "self-centered." Yet, if you don't tell the world who you are and what you want, how can the world help you? Hire you? Or advocate for you? It's time to take the shame out of shameless self-promotion.

Your personal brand is a platform that can allow you to do very special things; and the second you stop believing that it's wrong to advocate for or promote yourself is the exact same second you can get to work.

IDGAF

I hate to break it to you, but people already don't like you. People are already talking about you—and people are already judging you. Once you realize this, the question becomes not "What will these people think of me?" but rather "Who are you living your life for—you or them?" If they are already talking about you, you might as well give them something to talk about!

Remember in high school when you were so worried about being cool? You tried hard as hell to fit in and go with the flow and played along liking what everyone else did because it was way more safe to do the cool thing than to do your own thing. While that may have worked in high school before you knew any better, that's not how you should live your life. Not only is it okay to do "your own thing," you actually need to! We need more people in this world who are brave enough to live an authentic life—and to say "IDGAF"—"I don't give a f*ck." This means having the courage to be who you really are rather than being who you think the world wants you to be.

For so long I "hid" the hip-hop-loving side of my personality in business, thinking that no one would hire me if I liked rap music. Yet, this is who I am. I love all music, but especially love hip-hop. The second I said, "to hell with it," and started infusing my love of hip-hop into my work, my talks, my writing, and my social media, I started making more genuine connections. I also started attracting really cool clients and companies who also have a similar vibe, which makes the work I do as a speaker and writer even more rewarding. This is what you want: to work with and be around people who get the real you, not some BS version of yourself you put out there.

When you are out there doing something that matters to you, you are bound to tick someone off. There will be people who don't "like" you. Bless them and move on! The world needs you out there doing your thing. There is nothing more inspiring than watching someone come alive and step into their power.

As the CEO Fear Boss running the business of you, it's time to make waves, kick shame to the curb, and OWN IT.

OWN IT

We miss so many powerful and profitable opportunities because we are afraid. Maybe it's that promotion, or a raise—all of it gets missed because we lack the courage to go for it. If you were seated at a dinner table next to the CEO of your actual company, would you be able to tell them what you have accomplished at work? If you finally got the meeting with the client you have been dying to land, would you be able to explain to them why they need to work with you? We have to be able to brag on ourselves, and being prepared helps us toot our own horns—without blowing it.

I have always kept a "brand brag" in my back pocket. For example, when I was working a full-time job in corporate America, whenever I was at dinner next to a senior leader in my company or at a networking event with the boss, I had this "brand brag" framework memorized that I would use to put myself out there.

It works like this:

Hi! I'm _____ (first, last name)

Working in _____ (your position/role)

I'm so excited to tell you that recently I _____
(1 brag or accomplishment at work)

This helped _____ (who did it help?)

So that _____ (how did it impact the bottom line?)

Thank you for _____ (close with a brag on them and an acknowledgment of their leadership)

This ends up coming out in conversation like this: "Hey, Karen, great to see you. I'm Judi Holler from your Chicago-based sales and marketing team. I have to tell you we just closed $300K for the fourth quarter because we hosted that client event at Navy Pier! This helped our team make our annual goal so that we can continue to do this work we love. Thank you for valuing these customer experiences and giving us the budget for them; they really work!"

This is an easy way to show your value and become more memorable. Spend some time collecting a few "brand brags" you're proud of. Maybe it's money you saved the company, or a new revenue you found, or the talent you are retaining. Find something that stands out and showcases how badass you are! Be ready. It's up to you to brag on yourself and stand out!

HOW ARE YOU STANDING OUT?

Besides preparing your "brand brag," what are you doing *inside* your organization to stand out?

A friend of mine works in sales for a large food company. He is always a top performer, very visible in his territory with his customers, yet he couldn't get the promotion he kept trying for and very much deserved. He noticed that while all his customers knew and loved him out in his territory, his remote position made visibility inside his organization harder to get. So he decided to start bossing up on himself *inside* the organization by doing things that would bring him greater visibility, like asking to run a breakout session at the annual event, sitting on panels, sharing articles with his leadership, and scheduling time with them. Next thing he knew, he got that promotion he had been seeking. Why? Because he grabbed himself a seat at the table, showing his company who he is and why he rocks.

In order to stand out at your company, think of new ways that you can contribute. Here are a few ideas to get you thinking:

- Lead the next internal team meeting.
- Share concepts from books you read or conferences you attend.
- Lead a breakout or sit on a panel at your annual conference.
- Mentor someone.
- Share blogs and resources with your leadership.

- Rock a "brand brag" any chance you get with your leadership.
- Ask for time on your senior leadership's calendar and show up prepared with one thing you'd like to discuss.
- Make sure your leadership knows if you win an award or get recognized for your volunteerism outside the company.

These actions require some hustle on your part, and even more, the courage to do things differently. This effort will allow you to build job security and stay relevant inside your organization so when push comes to shove, you are top of mind and become the one senior leadership can't live without. When you understand that it's NOT shameful to promote yourself and that it's NOT shameful to want to do that, you can finally start getting out of your way.

LET'S GET GOOGLELICIOUS!

Promoting yourself inside your organization is a big deal, yet it's equally important to be doing things *outside* your organization as well, to build a platform that creates stability and opportunity for yourself. You have to constantly think: Do people know me? Do people even know what I do? Am I visible? Am I finding ways to stay company smart AND industry smart? Am I articulating the things that make me valuable? When push comes to shove, am I the one they can't live without?

All of these questions can be covered when you are regularly putting yourself out there, both inside and outside your organization. They can also be answered in a quick internet search.

Like it or not, Google is the new resume. Before anybody works with you, hires you, refers you, or collaborates with you, they're Googling you. Period. Right now, stop reading for a second and grab your smartphone or open your laptop. Go to Google and type in your name. What pops up? Do you even show up? Are you proud of what you see?

When you are visible online by providing value and contributing, you build trust, which can open doors to new possibilities, new clients, and new opportunities. Here are a few external self-promotion ideas that will help your Google search results:

- Volunteering in your community

- Sitting on industry boards

- Winning awards for your volunteerism

- Writing articles for industry publications

- Being active on social media

- Starting a blog

- Publishing articles on LinkedIn

- Getting out in your territory and making sure clients know you

You have to find ways to contribute so that when we Google you we see that you are active, engaged, and trustworthy. Your personal brand is a platform that can allow you to do very special things. This platform is your visibility; it's how we see you showing up, both inside and outside of work, and this is a critical part of staying relevant.

If you are anyone who has anything to say or sell, you need a platform. If we can't see you, we can't help you. As CEO of you, it's critical that you are doing things on the regular that advance your visibility. You have to promote yourself. This takes courage to put yourself out there; be proud of who you are and what you do!

How to Make Fear Your Homeboy
AND BE THE CEO OF YOU LIKE A #FEARBOSS:

1. Use a goal-focused planner.

If you don't schedule your priorities, someone else will. A goal-focused planner can help you work in 30-day windows (30 Rocks!) so you can get, and stay, strategically focused on your dreams, goals, and desires. There are many planners out there to choose from, so take some time to research "goal-focused planners" and see what may work for you. I personally use the VOLT Planner by Ink+Volt, and I love it. Other popular planners include: The Self Journal by BestSelf Co., The Full Focus Planner by Michael Hyatt, and The Commit 30 Planner.

2. ID your superpowers.

Have you spent any time lately thinking about the pillars that represent who you *really* are? Take some time this week to white space for an hour and really think through what your brand "superpowers" are. Here are a few questions that can help spark this self-reflection:

- How do you provide value?
- What are you proud of?
- What do you do better than anyone else?
- What can you shamelessly take credit for?

3. Have a swag statement.

Once you have identified your superpowers, you now need to tell us what those are! You are so much more than your job title. While your business card may say Director of Sales or VP of Marketing, that doesn't tell us what you really do and who you really are. Here is an easy framework I adapted, from a video by Michael Hyatt, to help you quickly articulate what it is that YOU do:

I am a _____ (your superpower or expertise)

who helps _____ (client or target audience)

understand or do _____ (what is the unique solution only you provide?)

so they can _____ (transformation that happens after we've worked with you).

4. Get a seat at the table.

Get yourself involved in a business or industry association. Chair committees, write articles, join boards. This exposure is not only a great platform-builder, but you will also build an incredible network while learning skills you just can't on the job.

5. Hang with the "cool kids."

It's a knee-jerk reaction to mentor up. We seek out those more experienced than we are to show us the way. Yet a secret weapon these days is to also have a mentor fifteen to twenty years younger than you. This is how you not only stay connected to pop culture but also keep in touch with the trends and know what's coming down the social pipeline. The added bonus of a younger mentor? It will keep you young. You are only as old as you feel. Look around you—are you surrounded by people your age, or are you seeking out the energy of youth to inspire you?

Don't forget to share your #FearIsMyHomeboy moments on social! Tag me and use the hashtag when you make any of these boss moves. I want to celebrate with you!

CHAPTER 5

Find Your Tribe and Love Them Hard

"The fastest way to change yourself is to hang out with people who are already the way you want to be."

—REID HOFFMAN

I f you think about your life and the opportunities you've had, you can probably think of more than a dozen people who have helped you. We never get anywhere alone. Without a doubt you've probably had a hero who inspires you, a mentor who has guided you, a teacher who made you push harder, and a coach who gets you to the finish line. Maybe this person is a friend or a family member, or even a spiritual advisor, scripture, or a book. We never get anywhere alone. If you want to make fear your homeboy, you can't do it alone. Your tribe is a powerful asset in managing your fear because in your scary moments, they will be there to pick you up and help you hit the reset button.

Up to this point we've talked about loving yourself, trusting the process, finding balance, and being the CEO of you. You have leveled up on yourself, and now you have to level up on your next challenge: building your team. People control all the resources, opportunities, and information in the world. I'm talking about ordinary people—good, old-fashioned, nice-to-meet-you, let-me-shake-your-hand kind of people. If you are looking for an opportunity, you are really looking for a person.

Life Is a Party

Welcome to the party of life! It's your party, which means you get to decide what kind of food you'll serve, what type of music you'll play, what you'll serve to drink, where the party will be, what time it starts, and a host of other things.

When you think of your life as a party, with people, experiences, and ideas you get to invite in, your perspective of how you move through all the day-to-day regular stuff changes. Because parties are fun, it's a reminder to have a little more fun in your life. It's also a reminder that there are a ton of choices in your life and you have some control over things, like your party's guest list.

WHO TO INVITE

People stand on the other side of any opportunity you are seeking. Maybe it's a raise, the promotion, the job, the speaking opportunity, the business you want to start, the resource you need: all of it requires other people. Additionally, the quality of your life experiences is determined by the quality of people in your life. When you consider this idea as you navigate your life, you start to make more intelligent decisions about who you seek out and who you invite into your life party. Having and keeping quality relationships in your life requires courage, self-love, and most certainly trust.

Think about this for a minute . . . every day you are trusting in others. You are trusting in your team, expecting that they will deliver on their promises. Trusting in your family, that they will be there for you. Trusting in your partner, that they will be faithful. Trusting that the bank will protect your money. Trusting that your kids will make the right choices. Trusting that your pilot will land the plane safely.

When I started studying and performing improv at the Second City Training Center Conservatory, every time I stepped out onstage it felt like I was doing a trust fall. I would be scared out of my mind, standing up on that stage, just hoping my ensemble would catch me. And they did—every damn time. Whether we bombed or we rocked, it was always a comfort to know that I had this group of people who were in this scary improv thing with me.

You need people in it with you too. Your guest list should consist of mentors, coaches, heroes, authors you read, inspiring people you follow on social, lifelong friends who are family, people you share a passion with, and colleagues who lift you up. There is safety in numbers, and knowing that you are not alone can be a badass way to manage your fear.

Spend some time assessing your tribe members. After spending time with them, do you feel depleted or recharged? Are they a positive force or are they energy vampires? Are they happy for you or manipulative? Do they take from you or do they give to you? Fear absolutely loves it when you don't have the courage to cut negative people out of your life. Why? Because these people will keep you stuck and miserable, which is exactly what fear wants.

You can't build a badass life with any of these negative emotions ruling your mind. As Iyanla Vanzant once said, "Sometimes you will have to meet people where they are and sometimes you will have to leave them there." Real talk: you are not responsible for the happiness of everyone around you. It's not sustainable, fun, or healthy to always be worrying about and taking care of everyone. People must show up for themselves; you can't save anyone else. You can inspire and encourage, yet you cannot hold yourself hostage for someone else's happiness.

You can inspire and encourage, yet you cannot hold yourself hostage for someone else's happiness.

A brave, badass Fear BOSS knows how to do this. To love yourself enough to know when it's time to let someone go. It's hard. It hurts. And it's scary as hell. Yet, when you remember that this is YOUR party, that you are in control of the invitations, and that most importantly, the quality of your daily interactions shapes the quality of your life, the decision to cut negative people out of your life becomes so much easier. Bless them and move on.

COACHES, MENTORS, AND HEROES . . . OH MY!

One thing most high achievers have in common is that they all seek out help. A lot. Every day. They see this investment as the cost of doing business because they realize that anyone who's ever done anything amazing never gets there alone. High achievers invest and spend time cultivating a network of people smarter than they are, different from them, and more connected than they are. This is done when you put in your time, stay patient, and make genuine connections with others by providing value and building trust.

Fear holds you back here because fear makes you tell yourself stories like: "I don't have time for that," or "I want it now," or "hiring a coach is a waste of money," or "the person I want to mentor me is way too busy; there is no way they will have the time." Now it's likely some of this is true, some of the time . . . but most of it is only another excuse fear uses to keep you stuck in "getting ready" mode.

If you want to level up, you need people to help you. A coach, or a mentor, or a hero can be a great source of insight and opportunity.

Let's break this down a little so you can understand how to utilize all three.

Coaches

A coach is someone who has done what you seek to do, or has helped others do what you seek to do. Because they have years of experience, they have a set of skills worth paying for.

It's not uncommon for people who are already established in their fields to seek a coach: bodybuilders hire fitness trainers; actors hire performance coaches; and entrepreneurs hire business coaches. Having someone outside your head and outside your everyday business who has no "personal" attachment to the end result to guide and push you can help you move through fear and stay in forward momentum.

Coaches typically run a business that offers their time and brain power. A coach will usually work with a client to create a structured program to help them advance their dreams and goals. Having a professional coach can be your step to real transformation, because when you are paying someone, you tend to take your preparation, time, and focus more seriously.

Mentors

Like a coach, mentors are people you look up to professionally or personally who are doing, or have done, the things you seek to do. Unlike a coach, mentors do not sell their time and services. They likely have a full-time job or are running a business in the industry you seek to either enter or level up in. Which means you have to get creative because these people are BUSY!

These high achievers likely have very hectic schedules, lead teams, travel a lot, and have limited bandwidth. In order to get their attention, not only do you have to get creative, but you also have to be respectful of their time. The best advice I can give you on reaching out to a mentor you wish to have access to is: be ready and don't waste their time. Send them an email, or ask in person when you see them, one clear question that you really want their advice on.

I call this micro-mentoring—spreading your questions out one at a time, over time, so you don't bombard someone and overwhelm them. You could have multiple micro-mentors going on at one time, which allows you to get a range of different perspectives on what you seek to learn. Plus, if one person doesn't respond, you still have a few other eggs in the cooker. When engaging a potential mentor, the bottom line is this: come prepared and have your sh*t together. Be direct, clear, concise, and organized in your communications with them.

I've used micro-mentoring over my career to slowly build relationships, inch by inch, with people I seek to learn from. What started out as a question blossomed over time into a relationship. I also make sure the micro-mentoring is not one-sided; I always seek to provide value back where appropriate and look for opportunities to help them as well.

Heroes

Heroes are mentors and coaches, but rather than working with them directly, you learn from afar. Your heroes are likely people you have not met in person, but whom you look up to and are inspired by when fear wants to take over.

Most of my heroes are people I've never met. Brené Brown is my Beyoncé. Amy Poehler is my favorite funny girl. Ally Love and Robin Arzon inspire me to #BossUP on the Peloton bike. Mel Robbins keeps me thinking 5, 4, 3, 2, 1 . . . action! Marie Forleo is my spirit animal and reminds me that everything is figure-out-able. Seth Godin reminds me to go make things happen. Steven Pressfield is my fear doctor. They sit on the shelves of my office in the form of books or they are digitally available via social media, TED talks, and podcasts, and I feel their magic every time I am challenged or hit a roadblock.

You can work the magic of your heroes into your schedule, too, whether it's reading their books, watching a TED talk, or listening to a podcast. Taking one of these small actions every day will expand your network of people and ideas. You can then share what you learn with your network, building your own trust and value, which will make you look like a boss all around.

No matter how long you've been in business or how successful you think you are, having a coach, hero, or mentor is an incredible way to level up and stay focused. Use your network to help you (mentors), model others who are crushing it (heroes), and hire someone who has done it before to help you stay focused (coaches). Building these people into your "tribe" will also help you stay woke to the power of positive energy in your life and make it easier to uninvite the energy vamps.

WHO NOT TO INVITE: ENERGY VAMPIRES

Energy vampires are people who literally suck the life right out of a room and a space with their negative energy. If you think of your office, I bet you can imagine a few—the people who walk into the conference room and things immediately feel negative and awkward. You can probably identify a few in your personal life, too, like an in-law, a parent, a sibling, or a friend who is constantly negative and brings everyone down. You should avoid inviting these people to your party at all costs, because it's going to drain your energy, which can make you stressed, anxious, sick, or worse.

Remember the *SNL* sketch "Debbie Downer"? (If not, stop reading and Google it—trust me, it's worth it!) The sketch is about a family at Disney World, the "happiest place on earth," and Debbie Downer is part of the trip. Everyone is so excited and happy and positive, but every time someone shares something they are excited about, Debbie finds a way to say something to bring the group down. *Womp, womp.*

It's a brilliantly written sketch because it's so dead-on in its portrayal of an energy vampire—we all know a Debbie Downer or three. It's not only annoying, but that negative energy is contagious. You can catch bad energy as quickly as you can catch a cold. Just like good energy can keep you well, bad energy around you can make you sick.

You should make it a goal to have a zero-tolerance policy for negative people, places, and things. Energy vamps love when you are down, because they feed on the negativity and want you to stay down with them. Fear allows you to accept this behavior from other people, when you know deep down you shouldn't. Tosha Silver writes in her book *Outrageous Openness*: "If you can't tell whether someone is good for you when they're around, after you leave them note how you feel. Did they fill you or did they drain you?" If you are constantly out of juice, it's time to cut back or slowly exit the relationship. Bless them and move on.

Yes, you will have to deal with negative people; there's no escaping it. While this can be a gift in itself, teaching you the power of patience and grace, it's never acceptable to allow the negative behavior of others to steal your greatness. You need to set hard boundaries. Energy vamps should never be invited to your party.

WORK THE ROOM

You have to always be looking for creative ways to stand out and expand your network. It is not my job to remember you; it is your job to make sure I don't have a chance to forget you. This is how you build a network, a tribe that will support you, refer you, hire you, and promote you. This is how you find the people that will unlock your opportunities.

It is not my job to remember you; it is your job to make sure I don't have a chance to forget you.

Have you ever noticed at industry events, or association meetings, that the same people always clique up? Or, how sometimes a bartender spends all his time coddling his "regulars"? Think about your office environment. Do you lunch with the same people? Cliquing up is a problem because you'll never open new doors for yourself if you don't have new people walking into the door of your life party to begin with.

Remember, another human being is likely on the other side of anything you really want, so if you want to create opportunities for yourself and get noticed, you must work the room. This means you actively seek out opportunities to meet new people and that you have the courage to put yourself into an unfamiliar situation.

When you're at an event and you stay where it's safe and familiar, you miss opportunities to meet someone who just might change your life—by making an introduction for you, teaching you something new, or even giving you your next job. This method is how I put into motion my entire career as I now know it. Almost fifteen years ago I was invited to a networking lunch. I nervously accepted the offer, went, and instead of safely sticking like glue to the side of the badass friend who invited me, I broke away to work the room by myself. I knew that if I wanted anything to happen for me, I had to make it happen for myself. So I took a deep breath and ventured out into the crowd.

I saw this tall, gorgeous blonde woman in a fancy suit standing by herself near the iced tea and thought to myself, I should meet her! I went up, grabbed a tea, and introduced myself, having no clue that this simple hello was going to change the course of my entire life. The amazing Heather Allison Smith ended up hiring me two weeks later for my first-ever salaried sales job, and that job set into motion the rest of my life. To this day, Heather remains someone I look up to and serves as a reminder of how powerful one hello can be. If I hadn't had the guts to break away from the friend who invited me, I probably wouldn't even be sitting here writing this book, and I shudder at the thought of how many other opportunities I would have missed.

You have to be able to work a room. You need to be able to muster up the courage to walk into an event and not let fear get in your way. Instead of sticking to the same social interactions we're used to because we're afraid to put ourselves out there, we can create incredible opportunities for ourselves when we have the courage to get uncomfortable. Yes, it's scary . . . and it likely will never feel less scary. But we feel less fear in these unfamiliar situations by having a social script to help you work the room like a boss.

Flip the Script

You know how it goes . . . you walk into a networking event and the conversation script usually goes like this: "Hey, Denise, how are you?" . . . "Oh, I'm good. Just, you know, crazy busy."

Ugh. Crazy busy. It's all we seem to talk about. How "busy" we all are. This isn't really how you are. Besides, we're all busy. Yet, we keep asking the same questions that keep getting us the same responses. We stick to these boring social scripts because we are afraid to try something new.

If you want to stand out, get noticed, and make memorable connections, you have to flip the script. You have to stop participating in "small talk" and start leveling up your conversations so you can stand out at your industry events, networking events, trade shows, dinner parties, and social events. A few simple shifts to the questions you ask in any social situation will change the way you are remembered, expand your network, and help you connect in fun and unexpected ways.

If you want to stand out, get noticed, and make memorable connections, you have to flip the script.

After reading the book *Captivate: The Science of Succeeding with People* by Vanessa Van Edwards, I learned to use her "conversation sparkers" to have better networking results.[17] These are questions that use specific trigger words to give you a *new* social script that will help you spark better conversations and help you make more genuine connections. Inspired by her research, I decided to try out these conversation sparkers for myself. I wanted to see what would happen if I flipped the usual social scripts on their head and tried something new. Would I have more connections, a little more fun, and be more memorable?

I found that when I asked the usual "safe/boring" small-talk questions, I gave out hardly any business cards and had little to no social interactions. When I used the conversation sparkers, as suggested by Vanessa, I came back with

---

17   Vanessa Van Edwards, *Captivate: The Science of Succeeding with People* (New York: Portfolio, 2017), 60.

almost ZERO business cards, and made on-the-spot LinkedIn and social networking connections with multiple people. I found by making a few simple shifts in my language, I could not only put the fear of what to say at bay, but I could make stronger connections with the new people I was meeting.

Here are a few of Vanessa's suggestions that I used:

Instead of these safe/boring questions . . .	Ask these conversation spark questions . . .
How's work?	Are you working on anything exciting lately?
How are you?	What was the highlight of your day?
Where are you from?	So, what's your story?
Been busy?	Any vacations coming up?
What do you do?	How did you get into the industry?

For example, when you use emotionally charged words like "exciting," you trigger dopamine in the brain of the person you are talking with—you will literally watch their eyes light up when they talk to you! On the flip side, when you ask someone about work, like we always do, most of the time you'll trigger stress instead of excitement because they will think: *I should actually be at work, not at this event!* By focusing on questions that spark happy thoughts, you can change the conversation from a negative one to a positive one. This leaves you more memorable! Plus, people love talking about themselves, their families, and their travels.

Lean into questions that will help you learn more about who they are as a human being, and watch your interactions become much more engaging. You have to trust that you can have better conversations and make more genuine connections. All it takes is a little creativity, curiosity, and confidence to try this out on your own at your next event.

Now let's look at how we can take care of that network and make nurturing your network a part of your day-to-day operations.

Nurture Your Network

We are most inclined to reach out to someone in our network when we need something. This isn't necessarily a bad thing; it's a part of human nature that we want to help other people. However, if your network only hears from you when you randomly reach out because you need something, you hurt yourself more than you help yourself. People can feel the difference between a genuine request and a non-genuine request.

You have to be thinking about ways to cultivate your network always, not just when you need something. Look for opportunities to reach out when you can offer something instead of asking for something. You could share a blog, a talk, or a podcast episode you love. Maybe you share an idea you learned at the last conference you attended. You could even share a book or a product you just discovered. Each scenario lets your prospect, client, network, or colleagues know you are thinking of them, and genuinely want to stay in touch, by wanting to share something that can help them or their team grow.

Personally, I spend time each week checking in with people in my network I haven't spoken to in a while for no reason other than to say hello, share information, or be helpful in some way. When I was actively working in a sales role full-time, I always used books, ideas, and cool TED talks as a way to connect with my prospects instead of only reaching out because I needed them to do something for me. While this may take a little work on your part, it packs a big punch on the back end because it keeps you in touch with your network on a regular basis and builds trust.

Fear blocks us from doing things like this because fear makes us think we don't have the time. Yet, you do have the time (remember how we became more "balanced" in chapter 3?!). Giving your network a little time each week is a great way to let people know you see them, appreciate them, and value them. It will also increase your own value, as people see you as dependable, trustworthy, and smart.

DO YOU SEE YOUR PEOPLE?

Do you ever wonder why some companies have incredible loyalty from their staff and others have high turnover rates? Do you ever wonder why some leaders recruit the best talent while others can't get a good hire to save their lives? The one thing you can do as a leader to change the game is to *see* your people. Acknowledge them, encourage them, compliment them, coach them, and spend time with them. Work *with* your people, rather than having them work *for* you.

When you decide to lead as the great Oz that hides behind the curtain, or you don't hang out in the break room, you end up secluding yourself. This creates a great disconnect inside your organization. This disconnect can create bad energy, a toxic environment, and lead to increased turnover.

Oprah once said the question she is always asked when the camera stops rolling—whether it's an interview with an A-list celeb, a president, or a world icon—is the question: "How did I do?" Her aha moment was this: we all just want to be seen. We want to know that we matter, that we performed well. We want to be encouraged.

If you are in a management role, you have an incredible opportunity to be an encourager. Take time to see the people you lead. Let them know how they did and that the work they do matters. You can do this in your individual review meetings with your team members, at staff meetings, via a handwritten note, via email—pick your pleasure! Doing this will make you someone we *want* to work for (and with) vs. someone we have to work with. When you make the time to encourage others on your team, you help them level up and become less afraid to be more of who they really are. This creates a badass chain reaction of positivity in your work environment that encourages more authentic connections and fewer fear-based assumptions.

Hand*ups*, Not Handouts

You have an opportunity to be a fear role model to others. How exciting is that to consider? When you realize that your network sees you, it can help you do even more brave things. Knowing that people look up to you and want to learn from you can help you recognize that your story, skills, assets, and talents that have gotten you to where you are today can shape the outcome of someone else's life.

When you are sharing your assets like knowledge, resources, gifts, and talents to help others, it is a hand*up*, not a handout. Giving handouts is easy. They are the CliffsNotes version of a book, or an answer key for a test. Handouts are hacks, shortcuts, easy and safe . . . but the longcut is where all the gifts, the handups, live.

Handups come in all shapes and sizes. They're someone giving you your first job in an industry or recommending you for a promotion. A handup is when someone introduces you to someone else who can help you solve a problem or give you advice. A handup is when someone else gives you an opportunity, makes a connection for you, or gives you the encouragement you need to take action for yourself. The big difference between a handout and a handup is that a handup requires you to do the work, after things are put in motion for you. Handups encourage, inspire, motivate, and push someone forward. This is why handups can be scary. They require grit, hard work, and hustle in order for them to work. Handups are the opportunities that change your life if you are willing to accept the challenge.

As a high achiever, it's easy to get sidetracked as you get busier. You forget that it took lots of people helping you to get you to where you are today. Fear wants us to get so busy that we stay in our comfort zone and forget to help others or share our ideas, clients, and connections. Fear makes us worry and believe that there is not enough for all of us. Fear wants you to think that you'll get left with nothing if you share too much.

One of the bravest things you can do is help others do amazing things. When I started my speaking business, I was in a mastermind group with two other women who were also working at building new businesses. Each of us was so different, we were able to provide different perspectives and help each other in creative ways. It was so valuable and helpful. One of the coolest things we did was refer business to each other—and it made me so happy to introduce them to past clients of mine who ended up booking both of them, multiple times.

This was a handup. While I made the introduction for them and gave my stamp of approval, they did the work to eventually book the business and sell themselves as the right fit for the client.

This kind of cooperation and support isn't always the case. A lot of folks in business get fearful of sharing too much because they think someone will steal their ideas, or clients, or do better than they can do. If these kinds of people were in a mastermind group, nobody would get the sort of value that they were looking for because they would hold back information, ideas, and connections. Fear would get in the way, no one would level up, and eventually the group would disband. Same in a business environment. You have to realize the universe is abundant and there is plenty for all of us. And remember, no one else does things exactly the way you do them; and anything that comes from you will always be original because it came from you in the first place.

When you do things like this, trust in yourself enough to share your resources and make others look good. You'll end up not only helping someone else level up, you'll also bring even more abundance into your life and network.

Make Others Feel Confident: Buildups

Making others look good and feel confident is a cornerstone of improv theater. When an improv group is onstage, they have three main jobs: 1) to listen like a boss so all players know what the heck is going on; 2) to focus like a ninja so everyone can stay in the moment; and 3) to make the other person the improviser is playing with look amazing. Focusing on making others look good and feel confident can change the game for you professionally and personally. When you look for opportunities to make others feel empowered and look amazing, you can enhance your personal brand inside your organization and industry, which ends up creating more opportunities for you because you become someone we trust and respect.

When you are brave enough to put yourself aside for a minute and support someone else's success, you become a fear role model. There are many small, but important, ways that you can help others look good and build confidence. You could send an email to the president of the company after someone else on your team does something positive, sharing the story (don't forget to include your teammate!). Or, you could write an unexpected note to the boss of someone who made your day or did something awesome for you. You could even just tell someone who works for you why they rock and how much you appreciate the value they bring to your organization.

We all need someone who is in our corner, someone to cheer us on and encourage us. It's easy to assume that because someone is crushing it, they are settled and don't need any extra support. It's equally as easy to only spend time developing our newer colleagues and to forget about our rock stars. We have to check in on our strong players as much as we do those who are having a tough time or are new. In college I did these things called "buildups" with one of my best guy friends. If we were down, worried about a test, had a bad breakup, or were just going through anything tough or scary, we'd call each other and say, "Okay, it's time for a buildup." Then our conversation would go something like this:

"You got this; you're the sh*t."

"Do you realize who you are? You are Judi motherf*cking Holler!"

"Go for it."

"What are you afraid of? You own this!"

We would get loud and use naughty language for drama and effect (imagine a coach in a locker room pumping up his players at halftime), and it always worked. Not only was it just as fun getting a buildup as it was dishing one out, but both of us would feel confident and supported afterward. It felt good to remind someone of *why* they are amazing and to get in their face about how badass they are.

Life can be hard and tough and scary. We get in our heads, then doubt and second-guess ourselves. Even the toughest of the tough need a buildup from time to time. Fear has a little army of soldiers just waiting to pounce when you start doing amazing things. You need your own squad, and you need to take care of that network, but you need to realize that fear also has a squad. And fear's squad is strong and relentless and always ready. Let's make sure you're ready to disarm them the second they show up.

Fear's Squad

A huge help in managing your fear is knowing how fear shows up. Just like you need to have a tribe and you need to nurture that tribe, fear also has a tribe and he works overtime nurturing it. Fear can get way more done this way; it allows Fear to trick you because sometimes you don't realize its peeps have shown up to your party with the sole intention of trashing it. This knowledge can become your power and help you stand up to these bullies.

Do you remember the musical *West Side Story*? There is this scene where the two street gangs, the Sharks and the Jets, face off in an epic dance battle to determine who's the best in the neighborhood. Your squad and fear's squad are like two rival gangs. Neither one of you wants to surrender, both of you think you're the best, and even if you're dancing your butt off, things can get nasty. You've got to sort it out. You and fear need to figure out how to work together and live in the same hood with peace. You can learn how to live with fear and his gang and thrive even when they show up.

MEET FEAR'S BFFS

Fear's squad has powerful members, and each one will manifest differently based on who you are. Here are a few of fear's BFFs:

Perfectionism	Drama
Procrastination	Gossip
Self-doubt	Anxiety
Self-sabotage	Change
Criticism	Excuses
Judgment	Blame
Self-medication	

Knowing that these feelings are connected to fear can help you manage them more effectively because any time you find yourself going down one of these self-destructive emotional rabbit holes, you can ask yourself the real question: What am I afraid of? The truth of the matter is this: the real reason fear's BFFs show up is to stop you so that you don't change or grow or level up. Because when you level up, you get stronger; and the stronger you get, the less you let fear boss you around.

When you see yourself procrastinating, stop yourself and call it for what it is: fear. When you start making excuses for why you don't have time, you can stop that behavior and call it for what it is: fear. When you see yourself paralyzed with self-doubt, you can stop the trash talking and call it for what it is: fear. By realizing that the most negative emotional behaviors you feel are really fear's BFFs trying to stop you from bossing up, you get a lot more confident when you tell them to hit the road.

FEAR-IDENTIFYING ROADMAP

When you are working on untangling your feelings and confronting your fear, let yourself off the hook a little because it IS scary. Say hello to the feeling and recognize it as fear. Then allow yourself to go to the worst-case scenario for a minute. What is the worst that could happen? Sure, you could die; but aren't we all dying already? It's highly unlikely you will actually die, in most cases, so what are the other worst-case things? And more importantly, what GOOD could happen too? Vocalizing these fears actually allows you to identify how your feelings are connected to fear and helps you rationalize your situation.

Grab a piece of paper and work through this exercise:

What am I freaking out about? _____

Worst-case scenarios	Positive things that can come out of worst-case scenarios	How will I recover from worst-case scenarios?	Who can help me recover from worst scenarios?

The moment you get your scary thoughts out of your head and down onto paper, you will see that most times the things you are afraid of aren't that big of a deal to begin with, and that they are manageable. This exercise helps you take back your power from fear and stay in control. While you may still be afraid, you have a new perspective that allows you to remain focused on moving forward—and keep moving forward, one day at a time.

You will feel fast fears that hit you like a ton of bricks; you will feel slow fears that creep up gradually over time. These fears arise especially as you continue to level up. Scary stuff will happen; you will feel lost, you will feel out of control, and you may even go down the doom-and-gloom black hole. Putting pen to paper, leaning on your tribe, and focusing on the positive are all tools to disarm fear's squad. And this gets easier the more you practice it. Plus, each decade of your life will present you with different fears; and overcoming each new fear is another step in your journey.

In Conclusion

Your tribe is a lifeline, personally and professionally. Now that you know you are in control of who comes to your life party, you even the playing field. While you can't fully escape all negative people, places, and things, you can do your best to avoid energy-sucking situations anytime you have a choice. And when you can't manage this, you can decide to let fear become your teacher by asking yourself, "What is this here to teach me?" and by reminding yourself, "I'm the boss, not fear or this energy vampire." This perspective puts you in control, not fear. Fear also has a network, a squad, a tribe . . . and they are ready. Ready to stop you from leveling up and being the badass you were destined to be. Don't let them!

How to Make Fear Your Homeboy

AND NURTURE YOUR TRIBE LIKE A #FEARBOSS:

1. Make others look good.

You can do this at work by asking yourself a series of questions I call my "Boss Up" questions. These questions will keep you focused on contributing rather than blending in. At the end of every week, ask yourself, "Did I Boss Up by…"

- making contributions to discussions or adding value in my meetings and conference calls this week?

- making life easier, more successful, for my leader, boss, or manager?

- acknowledging the great work of teammates or colleagues by reaching out to thank them?

- publicly praising others for their contributions (especially in front of their boss)?

- creating and publishing content (a blog, video, article, infographic, etc.), breaking down the information that will be useful to people in my network?

- integrating my superpowers (the things I do better than anyone else) into everything I did?

- sharing content created by others (articles, blogs, YouTube videos, etc.) that will be valuable to members of my network, while adding my unique point of view to the content I shared?

- reaching out to at least three members of my network with the goal of nurturing those relationships?

2. What would Oprah do?

Think of your heroes. Maybe it's Oprah, or Brené Brown, or Seth Godin, or God, or Jesus, or yo' mama . . . or maybe, like me, it's Marie Forleo! When you get overwhelmed, stressed, frustrated, or out of sync, take a deep breath and ask yourself, "What would [insert hero] do?" It's so simple and a little silly, but it can really work. This simple perspective shift can help you act "as if."

For example, say someone said or did something super hurtful to you. You would go instantly to your happy place and say to yourself, "Okay, what would [your hero] do?" Then you will shift your perspective and put yourself in the positive space of someone you look up to. How would Marie, or Brené, or Oprah handle this? Would they lash out? Nope. Would they hide? Nope. Would they react? Nope. This will help you check yourself before you wreck yourself and put your headspace into the clouds a little with someone you admire.

3. Run your own conversation sparker experiment.

Take the spark questions presented in this section and use them at the next industry event to run your own experiment! Pick four team members and divvy up the questions—with half the team asking the safe questions and half asking the spark questions—and see what happens. Are you making more connections? Are you getting asked for your business card more? Are you becoming memorable? Are you getting on-the-spot LinkedIn or Facebook connections? What conversation sparkers did you invent or create that pack a big punch?

4. Avoid the question you should never ask.

When seeking out time with a mentor, there is one thing you should never do: ask to "pick their brain." Most people don't have time to "meet you for coffee" or let you "pick their brain." The mentor you seek out likely has a million plates spinning, and an ambiguous email to "pick their brain" will typically get deleted from an inbox without guilt. Here are a few ideas to get you thinking creatively if there is someone you really want to learn from:

- Ask one pointed, well-thought-out question you're really interested in and that you know this person may have a perspective on. Nine times out of ten you'll get a thoughtful and valuable response. Most of us have time to answer a specific question.

- If you do get time with a mentor you seek out, like a meeting or coffee in person, have a plan. Build an agenda on what you'd like to cover, and send two to three bullet points to the mentor in advance. The mentor will not only appreciate it and be very impressed, but you will also be able to make the most effective use of their time, which builds incredible trust.

5. Manage energy, not spreadsheets.

You spend a lot of time at work managing budgets and spreadsheets and strategic plans, all in an effort to protect the tactical assets in your day-to-day business operations. Do you ever think about protecting the *energy* of your people? Keeping the energy in your office positive not only keeps your colleagues happy, but it also can lead to greater retention and productivity. Employees leave leaders, and organizations, when they don't feel seen. It's natural for us to want to exit negative situations. How can you expect your organization to thrive if the people inside it are miserable?

To help you assess the energy of your colleagues and team, spend time with them and try asking things like:

- What do you need to learn?

- How do you prefer to get information?

- Are you extroverted or introverted?

- What are your sleep patterns?(This will help you determine their optimal performance hours.)

- Do you prefer to work in groups or solo?

- When are you most creative?

- Are you a visual learner or more hands-on?

- What motivates you?

Don't forget to share your #FearIsMyHomeboy moments on social! Tag me and use the hashtag when you make any of these boss moves. I want to celebrate with you!

CHAPTER 6

The Magic of Momentum

"There's nothing as unstoppable as
a freight train full of f*ck-yeah."
—JEN SINCERO

Forward momentum is everything. If fear has an archrival, it's action. Knowing that action—moving forward even when you don't think you can—is your secret weapon in managing your fear allows you to slice through worry, doubt, and anxiety because fear loses its power once you pick up momentum. See, it's not that you can't do scary things; it's that you *don't*.

When was the last time you purposefully did something to scare yourself a little? Maybe it was raising your hand to lead the next sales meeting, or asking for a raise, or going to a SoulCycle class, or speaking up on the conference call, or having the tough conversation with a friend. These things can feel small, but they are gigantic steps forward. Think about turtles for a second: little, cute, slow-as-molasses turtles. They are incredible fear role models. In order to move forward, literally, these turtles have to leave the comfort of their shells and stick their necks out. Turtles can only make progress when they are brave enough to come out of their safe place and see what's going on around them. If they don't do this, they risk staying in the same place forever, never seeing the world around them, starving to death, and risk becoming prey themselves.

The same goes for you, Fear BOSS! If you want to do anything amazing, if you want to level up, if you want to have a comfortable life . . . you have to leave the comfort of your shell. You have to stick your neck out from time to time, look at what's going on around you, and decide where you want to go next. The more you do this, the easier it gets, and the braver you become.

Yet too often we stay stuck inside. Instead of poking our necks out and moving ahead, we wait. We stay nice and warm and cozy in our turtle shells waiting for a better time, the right amount of experience, more money, or better connections. All of these things we are waiting for are simply manifestations of fear. Fear is holding us back, making us question everything.

Fear is trying to make us forget that there will never be a right time—there is only right *now*.

You want to leave that job you've been "stuck" at for fifteen years? Start looking for new opportunities and working your network.

You want to lose the twenty pounds you gained post-baby? Start walking around your neighborhood.

You want to write a book? Start writing.

You will never be ready; no one ever feels truly "ready." This is why you must start BEFORE you are ready. If you are sitting around waiting for things to be perfect—for more resources, more experience, more knowledge—before you start, you'll be waiting a long time. Real talk: perfect doesn't exist, and anything that you feel looks perfect only got that way because someone had the courage to start in the first place. When you start, the badass side effect is that you will organically receive more experience, more knowledge, and more resources simply because you started.

Think about our turtle friends. If they waited for when they were ready to come out of their shells, they'd never move an inch. Instead, they know they need to come out in order to find water, feed, mate, and stay alive. You gotta move, Fear BOSS! When you take action, the party officially begins. Action becomes the most popular person at your life party, and its main goal is to show you the ropes and help you boss up.

No one is ever "ready." You must start BEFORE you are ready.

THE DANGEROUS "GETTING READY" STAGE

Fear loves when you are in the "getting ready" stage, because it's easy to keep you there. Whether you're asking for more time to finish a project, thinking you need to get another year of experience under your belt, saying that you'll start the business next year when you have more money saved, or putting off quitting your job until after you're married, each of these "conditions" is actually an excuse. This is fear getting in your head and saying, *You are not ready yet.*

Which is all BS. You don't need any of these made-up requirements to start working toward your goal; the only thing you need in order to stop "getting ready" is momentum.

Momentum is more powerful than you may realize because it means increasing forward motion. A boulder rolling down a hill picks up forward momentum as it goes. Teams on a winning streak, great ideas, and the economy can also gain momentum. The second you go from "getting-ready mode" to "I'm-ready-to-slay mode," you will experience the powerful energy of momentum. Momentum is a physics term that refers to the quantity of motion an object has. It is mass in motion. The greater the mass, the greater the motion. You hear this all the time in sports. Once a team picks up momentum, they are "on the move" and hard to stop. It's an energy shift that happens mentally and physically. Players feel it, coaches feel it, fans feel it. Remember Newton's first law of motion?

Newton's law says that any moving object will continue to move forward unless it's interfered with. This idea applies to momentum as well. Once you start taking action, you invite momentum to the party, and momentum rarely wants to leave. Fear knows that the only way to stop you and your momentum is to mess with you and interfere (or should I say interFEAR) with you . . . so fear will show up in a panic to make you stop. Fear will pull out all the stops (self-doubt, self-sabotage, anxiety, and excuses) at this stage, because momentum means you are there, you are in motion, and fear is always strongest at the finish line.

Momentum's energy propels you forward. It's like the universe's way of pushing you onto the karaoke stage, or off the diving board. Of course fear would much rather you continue to keep getting ready, because perpetually getting ready means you haven't done anything yet.

I know a badass budding female entrepreneur who has a killer business idea. It's fresh, it's original, it's authentic to who she is, it's her passion, and the world needs it! Yet she's stuck in this "getting ready" phase. She feels she can't start because she needs the perfect business cards, the right logo, the slick website, one more class, one more month, and on and on and on the list of excuses goes. Guess what happened? Someone else beat her to it and is now dominating the marketplace with the exact same idea.

This person didn't steal her idea; this person is fully qualified as well and has the same passions, experience, and fresh content. The only difference is one person started, while the other stayed safe in her shell. I don't know about you, but if there is one thing that scares the hell out of me, it's regret. When you wait, when you get stuck "getting ready," that's what you get. Regret. You must love and trust yourself enough to know that you must go scared.

Do It Scared

When was the last time you did something for the first time? It's natural to think, "Okay, this is scary" or "I'm afraid to do this," so we don't. We wait. We stall. And sometimes we stop all together. Fear is such a pervasive part of our lives that you may think you need to get rid of it in order to begin working toward your goals. However, you can't outrun your fear, and it's not something you can beat. You will never be fearless, but you can get really good at fearing LESS—and by that I mean you have to do the work and do things when you're scared.

This really is your first step. Understanding that you must go scared. Then, once you wrap your mind around this idea of going scared, you can start to really think through the things you want to do and why you're not doing them in the first place. Is it fear? Or is it because you legit don't want to do it? Take some time to think about what it is that you *really* want. More money? More health? Love, marriage, kids? A promotion? A degree? Get clear on what you want and then start to think about *why* you aren't getting it. I'd bet my bottom dollar the answer to that Q is the fact that you aren't taking action. And because of this, momentum can't find you.

Take public speaking, which is pretty much a fear for most people. Many people are terrified at the thought. The only reason anyone gets comfortable speaking in public is because they do it again and again, over and over. So while you may feel nervous and scared as you do something that you're afraid of, know that you will get braver with experience. Confidence comes after repeated experiences of making it through the scary thing. You do the thing once, it goes well, then you do it again. Next thing you know, you have figured out how to do it afraid. You'll be comfortable with your fear, because you'll be familiar with it as part of the action you've learned to take.

When was the last time you did something for the first time?

I speak for a living, and I am afraid every time I step onstage. Yet I've learned that about five minutes into any speech or emcee job, my fear is gone. Poof! I'm already in too deep with action, so fear has no place to go. It's pretty incredible, really. Fear's power is gone because I've put one foot in front of the other, stepped out onstage, and done the scary thing anyway—which gives me momentum! The same will be true for any action you'd like to get better at, like speaking, writing, dating, or any other skill you'd like to develop. Confidence comes with surviving, and even succeeding, despite your fear.

Yes . . . AND I'd Love to Fear-LESS

As written in one of my favorite business books on improv, *Yes, And,* authors Kelly Leonard and Tom Yorton of Second City report that Dr. Mark Pfeffer, a psychotherapist and director of the Panic/Anxiety Recovery Center in Chicago, says: "Every time you learn to be unafraid, your brain changes. [Improv is] the quickest way to get to the neural pathway change, because it puts [people] in a situation where they're facing their fears."

Improv is like fear yoga for your soul. It's a solid, strength-building fear exercise that can help you get more zen with your fear. You start to learn that while scary things will never get less scary, you *will* get stronger.

Saying "Yes, and" may be the most powerful strength-building secret of improvising, because it's how we keep our scenes in forward momentum onstage; and this momentum is what gives the improvisers confidence to keep building a scene together, one brick at a time. Improvisers are trained to say "Yes, and" in order to agree to the last thing that was said, validate the other player, and keep a scene moving forward. Saying yes is an act of courage in improv, and in life, because 99 percent of the time you have zero clue where that yes will take you, and that makes a lot of us nervous. In improv that yes could lead you to an epic failure or a hysterical scene onstage. Improvisers are ready for the risk either way, because they are trained to trust the process (which is the training and each other), and to trust themselves enough to know that no matter what happens, they will be okay. Our improv mantra is "No Mistakes, Only Gifts," which helps us slice through the scary feeling of not having control.

In real life, you are doing the same! You say yes to the new city, having no clue if you'll love its vibe or your new neighborhood. You say yes to the relationship, having no clue if it will end in love and marriage. You say yes to the new job, having no clue how long you'll work there or if you'll hit your goals. You say yes to the new workout class, having no clue if you'll like it or not. Each time you say yes to something, you are saying yes to move your life forward and that you trust (and love!) yourself enough to know that no matter what happens, you will be okay.

The "Yes, and" mindset is one that requires you to trust that others around you will support your ideas and input, and it equally requires that you will do the same for others, whether you like the initial idea or not. Words like "No" and "Yes, but" are super popular in work environments, and in life, because they allow one person to stay in control of an idea, conversation, or opportunity. When someone says, "I love you . . . BUT," you immediately forget how good the "I love you" part felt because the "but" part mentally triggers a negative reaction.

It's the same in any conversation. "Your presentation was great . . . but" . . . or "I really want to promote you . . . but" or . . . "Your idea for the department is great . . . but." Each scenario is non-supportive and negative in nature. Therefore, while you may not love or agree with every idea someone presents to you, you can still use the "Yes, and" idea to deliver a more positive message.

You can use this idea in many situations, for example: "Your presentation was great . . . AND next time let's use fewer slides!" Or this: "I really want to promote you . . . AND as soon as I can get my budget approved, let's put a plan together." And this: "Your idea for the department is great . . . AND I encourage you to keep thinking creatively!" See the difference? You can still "disagree" and add constructive feedback in a positive, supportive way. "Yes, and" allows you to turn your conversations into gifts that encourage your team, move things forward, and create a positive work environment.

Improvisers are trained to see mistakes and failures as gifts. When something bombs onstage for an improviser, it's natural to be excited about the failure and even to say: "*Yes*, we bombed tonight, *and* wasn't it great that we tried something new?" Saying yes allows the actor to share control, keep it positive, and make the person they are playing with look good. Same in business. Say you give a presentation that falls flat. Instead of crawling into a hole and never giving another presentation, you can think like an improviser and say, "Well, that didn't go as well as I planned . . . AND that's okay because I learned that I used too many slides, I should have rehearsed longer, and my opening needed a more relatable story." This mindset moves you out of fear and into a powerful, productive place so that next time you give a talk you can slay it.

As Ryan Holiday writes in *The Obstacle Is the Way*, "Failure really can be an asset if what you're trying to do is improve, learn, or do something new."[18] Problems can become opportunities. You can ask things like: What worked? What didn't? What went wrong? What am I missing? When you reframe failure this way, you remove the power fear has over you because you can see failures as experiments in bossing up.

IS IT A HELL YES, OR A HELL NO?

If you are reading this and feel lost, uninspired, confused, and have no clue what to do next with your life, here's an experiment to begin right now: start saying yes to everything that comes your way! Offers, plans, opportunities, dinner, drinks—whatever!

This is going to sound crazy, especially since I've advised you to seek out balance in your life by getting comfy saying no to things; yet if you are lost, feel

---

18   Ryan Holiday, *The Obstacle Is the Way* (New York: Portfolio/Penguin, 2014), 82.

behind, and aren't getting what you want out of life, you should try to say yes to as much as you can. Yes, I will. Yes, please. Yes, me! Yes! This advice is especially for you if you are new to a role, a company, or a career.

I learned early in my career that saying yes was a secret weapon. Yes, I'll go to that meeting. Yes, I'll join you for dinner. Yes, I'll chair that committee. Yes, I'll take that job. Yes, I'll mentor that coworker. This allowed me to test out so many new skills. I was scared, even if I'd agreed to take these new challenges on; but I was hungry to learn and get noticed.

I even have a few crazy yeses in there that shaped my story—like the time I flew to Chicago at the age of twenty-three to audition for MTV's "Wanna Be a VJ" competition. Now, this was back when MTV actually played mostly music videos and had VJs (aka video jockeys). I worshipped them! I got out of all my college finals, covered my shifts at the bar, flew to Chicago from St. Louis, and said *HELL YES*. I was scared to death, but my body was screaming, *You have to do this*. I stood in line for hours in the freezing cold rain until I finally got my chance to audition—and I bombed my final on-camera audition.

Now, even though I never did become an MTV VJ, this experience was still a success. I did not wait for someone to say, "Hey, come to Chicago and audition for this cool thing." Instead, I reached out and snatched it up for myself. I said yes. I learned I could travel alone, be alone, put myself in uncomfortable situations, take risks, fail, and *still be okay*. And I learned that if I wanted to do something, I had to go get it for myself.

Most of us say no more than yes because we are afraid, which can end up being the kiss of death personally and professionally. Really ask yourself why you're saying no. Is it because you are really protecting your time and don't have the bandwidth, or is it because you are afraid to put yourself out there and get uncomfortable? What can you reach out and grab for yourself? You have to say yes if you want to grow. You have to say yes to stand out. You have to say yes if you want to stay relevant.

CONTINUE SAYING YES

As we get older and more advanced, we have a tendency to stop saying yes. We think because we have experience, are in the C-suite, or have been in business for many years, that we know it all. So we don't join association committees, we don't attend as many breakout sessions at the conference, and we don't read as much. Who has the time, right? Well, we all should.

Saying yes is a requirement for leveling up, at any stage of your career. It's how we stay relevant, fresh, and young. It's how we get reenergized by working with and learning from those younger than we are and from people with different experiences. Saying yes is how we keep growing.

Be honest with yourself: Do you say yes, or is your default response "I'm too busy"? Do you put yourself in uncomfy situations? Are you open to learning from people younger than you, or do you feel like you're better—more experienced, perhaps—than they are?

Saying yes and being open to new things is a superpower. Same with balance in your life, as we learned in chapter 3. And I get what's going through your head right now; you're probably asking, How do I know when I should say yes and when I should say no? Here's my quick advice: take time to slow down your yes. This means instead of a knee-jerk reaction to the opportunity and immediately screaming "HELL YES" or "NO WAY," take twenty-four hours to think on it. It's amazing what a good night's sleep will teach you! Then, when you wake up, is it still a HELL YES, or has that yes turned into a no because you were able to step away and remove the emotion of it? If it should be a no, your entire body will react. You may get headaches, you may feel anxiety or stress, you get irritable, and often your body tightens.

On the other hand, yeses feel expansive; they scare and excite you at the same time; they open doors and push you outside your comfort zone. They are where the magic lives! You have to get uncomfortable if you want to grow, no matter what stage of your life and career. There is just no way around it. So be ready to say yes to the promotion, yes to giving the talk, yes to the new city, yes to the conference, yes to the new job, and yes to reading the book. Say yes, yes, yes!

ALWAYS BE READY

In improv theater we are told, "Always be alive on the back line." This means that when players are out front doing a scene, at any time another person could be "called in" to the scene, so all players have to be ready, regardless of whether they are onstage or not. This means that all of us have to be looking for opportunities to contribute and need to be listening so we are ready to say yes. You can use this improv idea in your professional life to stay relevant and stand out at work.

It is dangerous to "go through the motions" and hope something good will happen for you. In order to succeed, you have to take an active role in your life. You must always be ready—listening to what's going on around you. Not the drama, or gossip, or comparison, but really be aware of all the moving parts that make up your personal and professional life. Become alive in the scenes that make up your life, even if they are not "onstage" right now.

It's your job to stay alive on the back line. No matter how long you've been in your role or how much experience you have, you cannot check out. Going through the motions is the kiss of career death, and that energy tells your team, and those around you, that what you do doesn't matter to you.

What does it mean to be alive on the back line? At work it could mean that you find opportunities to help and contribute. You focus on your tasks, you see problems and find ways to solve them, you listen in meetings and take notes. You're alive on the back line when you stay present at an event or at dinner with a client by putting your phone away and by bringing positive energy to your interactions.

You have so much to contribute. These contributions can give you momentum and move your life and career forward. Momentum requires you to be ready so that when an opportunity presents itself you are able to JUMP on it because you are awake, engaged, and alive in the scenes of your life. You are ready to take action. It takes guts to stay alive on the back line, to always be ready, and to put energy into this idea. Remember: momentum is hard to stop once it starts, so be ready for it because you never know when it may show up.

Beta Bravery

It can feel hard to start or to move forward because you get overwhelmed. Looking at your big goal and seeing how far away the light at the end of the tunnel is—that's intimidating. Our brains start looking for ways to quit before we've even started.

We don't know where to start, so we don't. This is fear. Because the second you decide to earn that degree, or move to a new city—you will be happy—or at least on the road to being happy! These decisions *change* you, because they set motions into action. They are a source of momentum, and while they are the first step on the journey to achieving a large goal, they are small, important, and achievable steps.

Nearly all big, life-changing goals can be broken down by implementing what I call "beta bravery." This is taking the big thing you have to do and breaking it down into tasty little bite-sized chunks. Beta bravery is a magical little idea that destroys feelings of overwhelm because it helps your brain take the big, scary thing and chip away at it in manageable, easy pieces. Beta bravery also slices through stress, and anxiety, and illness, because it forces you to not do *all* the things . . . just the next thing. Improv lives in this space because it's not about the *best* thing in improv; it's always about the *next* thing. The most important question you can ask yourself on the regular is: Am I moving forward? Even if it's small, even if it's for five minutes, are you moving forward?

It's not about the best thing in improv; it's always about the next thing.

Take this book, for example. I mean, guys, a book! Although this has been a dream of mine for a while, I never quite knew how to start writing it because it felt so big, and hard, and overwhelming. I saw fear creeping up: *Where should I start? What should I say? Am I even a good writer?*

I invited beta bravery to the fear party. Once it was time to start writing, all I had to do was write one word. That word then became a sentence, and that sentence became a paragraph. Guess what? All of these small steps together became a book.

Beta bravery can work for you, too, if you focus on one step, one forward motion:

- You want to lose twenty pounds. Focus on losing one pound this week.
- You want to read more books. Start by reading ten minutes a day.
- You want to write a blog post. Set a timer for five minutes and write your first words.
- You want to get an advanced degree. Set aside one hour a day to study.
- You want to run a half marathon. Start by running your first mile.
- You want to get noticed by your leadership. Start asking the first question at every meeting.
- You want to get married one day. Start by going on a date.

Beta bravery will become one of your BFFs in managing your fear. These small steps will help you unlock your momentum.

SHORTCUTS VS. LONGCUTS

Why is everyone always in such a hurry? We are always in a rush for this or that: more money, more love, more fame, more "stuff"—and we want it now, now, now. But dreams and goals don't just happen overnight. You know these stories of people saying "She was an overnight success!" or "Wow, she came out of nowhere"? They aren't true. Things can take a long time to happen, and having to wait for the thing you are working toward isn't necessarily a bad thing. Momentum knows this, which is why it's so powerful; because by the time you have gotten some momentum in your life, you have really earned it!

No one comes out of nowhere. Most of the people you look up to have put in thousands and thousands of hours of work. There's really no shortcut to success. By the time this book is published, I'll have written hundreds of blog posts. I'll have delivered hundreds of keynotes to thousands of people at live speaking engagements all over the US. I'll have performed in hundreds of improv shows. I'll have recorded hundreds of videos teaching what I know. This book, it's the longcut. All the other stuff got me ready for it.

See, the shortcut is easy, quick. And if you aren't careful, it can be dangerous. When you are always chasing the shortcut, the hack, the quick fix, you rob yourself of critical opportunities to grow. You end up getting half the lesson you need. A shortcut is like taking a pill to cure a stress headache rather than focusing on balancing your schedule. Or fasting for three days to fit into a dress, rather than exercising and eating right regularly. A shortcut is almost always emotionally charged and shortsighted. It results in having to repeat the same lesson over and over, because you haven't learned the skill or technique to level up.

A longcut requires focus, patience, and sacrifice. When you're training for the marathon, a longcut looks like the six months of Saturday mornings where you were out logging miles instead of catching brunch with your friends. Or, it could be the years of speaking for free to build a network and reputation so you can land a paid gig. The longcut never gets easier, but it makes you stronger. It can feel like waiting, but it's really a long, steady period of growth.

If you feel rushed, and stressed, and always like you are in a hurry: stop and take a look at what is making you feel this way. You probably are trying to take a shortcut or advance something that may not be fully cooked yet, which is making you feel overwhelmed. Fear Boss, you gotta bake that cookie! I mean, I love me a fresh-baked, ooey-gooey cookie, but they easily fall apart. Bake the cookie all the way through and reap the delicious rewards of a perfectly done cookie that doesn't melt in your hands.

Betty Crocker aside, your life is worth more than a hack or a shortcut so you can rush through something. You deserve to enjoy all the success and growth and badassery that a longcut will give you. Let any momentum you achieve in your life be a shining symbol that you are exactly where you need to be and that the longcut is working.

In Conclusion

Embracing momentum requires you to shift your perspective on fear, but mostly it requires you to take action and start making waves. Big waves, small waves—it doesn't matter. The more action you take, the better you get; and the better you get, the more confident you will become.

Doing scary things never gets easier, but you will get stronger, more confident, more skilled, and more resilient. Fear wants you to keep putting things off, to keep making excuses. To stall. Pause. Overthink. Wait. The antidote to stuck, safe, and just the same is *starting*. The magic of momentum begins by leaning into your fear rather than trying to get rid of it.

How to Make Fear Your Homeboy
AND GET MOMENTUM IN YOUR LIFE LIKE A #FEARBOSS:

1. Try the ten-minute rule.

One of the best ways to start gaining momentum is by doing ten minutes of the thing you don't want to do. Remove all distractions, set a timer for ten minutes, and start. When the timer goes off, stop. If it feels good, keep going! If not, stop and do it again tomorrow. Usually you'll find that by the time you are ten minutes in to the thing you "don't want to do," you've invited momentum to the party, which makes it hard to stop because it feels oh-so-good!

2. Run your own fear experiments.

The goal of any fear experiment is to get uncomfortable, on purpose, and the more you do this, the more comfortable you will get being uncomfortable! Here are some fear experiments you can start using right now to strengthen your bravery muscle:

- Ask the first question in meetings or on conference calls.
- Raise your hand to lead the next team meeting or conference call.
- At the next party or networking event you attend, leave who you came with on purpose to meet new people.
- Use a conversation sparker at your next meeting or networking event.

- Ask for a discount or a free size upgrade at your coffee shop.

- Take selfies (of yourself) in public to get better at not caring what others think.

- Take an improv class!

3. Challenge your mind.

What have you always wanted to try? An improv class, Toastmasters, a new language, traveling alone, going to another country, karaoke, using a turntable, dancing the salsa? Make yo'self a plan and get started.

4. "Fear set" just like you "goal set."

When I watched Tim Ferriss's TED talk on his idea of "Fear Setting,"[19] I was quickly inspired to create a modified version of my own fear-setting exercise that I complete several times a year, as needed, for both personal and professional growth:

Dream or Goal: _____

Excuses for why you can't	What could go wrong?	How would you recover?	What's the cost of inaction?	What could go right?

---

19   Tim Ferris, "Fear-Setting The Most Valuable Exercise I Do Every Month," https://tim.blog/2017/05/15/fear-setting.

5. Give yo'self permission!

I'm officially writing you a permission slip to seek out more longcuts and let yourself off the hook from feeling FOMO or behind or rushed. You are allowed to take it slow. You are allowed to go at your own pace. And you are allowed to be exactly where you are.

Date _____

(Your name)_____ has permission to take the longcut. To go at her own pace and to learn all she needs to know in order to succeed on her own terms. (Your name)_____
will not worry about missing out or fear that she's too late because she knows that she is exactly where she needs to be at this moment, learning what she needs to learn.

Fear Is My Homeboy,

(Your signature)_____

@JudiHoller

CHAPTER 7

Your Homeboy, Fear

"The resistance is always strongest at the finish line."
—STEVEN PRESSFIELD

Have you ever been to a party that you wished would never end? The kind of party where you could stay all night, and you feel like sobbing when it's over? The kind of party that pumps energy into your bones and leaves you feeling rebooted, reminded, and recharged? Believe it or not, that fabulous party is the fear party, the one you joined as you began your journey through this book. And the good news is: you never have to leave it.

At the fear party, you've been introduced to all kinds of important things: self-love, a trusting universe, your inner CEO, your tribe, and your new best friend, action. Now it's time to make one last introduction—to the guest of honor: fear.

Most people avoid fear at the fear party, but not you, because now you know better. You realize that in order to make this the best party you've ever attended, fear has to feel welcome. Plus, you know something fear doesn't; you aren't afraid of it like everyone else is. You welcome fear into your house and pour it a drink, and you always have your eyes on the prize: freedom.

Embracing fear, as you have learned to do, gives you the freedom to be who you are and to do what you love. This means freedom to be present, because you've designed your life to have time for you to be that way. It's freedom to feel less anxiety, because you know the universe is abundant and always has your back.

You've been able to embrace fear and let freedom into your life because you've started to see yourself as an improviser. Every day, as you collaborate and solve problems, as you embrace mistakes as gifts and say "Yes, and," you have grown comfortable with not knowing how everything is "supposed" to go.

Life is improv. Being prepared, taking action, and being alive on the back line means that you've gotten really good at doing things while being afraid.

This shift in your perspective, living fearfully instead of fearlessly, is how you step into your power and your courage. And, dear fearful one, your courage will help you change your world.

The Never-ending Story

You will never get rid of your fear, and trying to get rid of it is the wrong approach. All you do when you try to outrun your fear is end up out of breath— you can't outrun it. Fear is a never-ending story that loves to creep back into your life just when you think you've gotten it "beat." This is actually great news, because fear shows up to keep you on your toes and remind you that you are very much alive! What a blessing that is!

Think about a situation in your life where you feel fear. Maybe you're afraid of flying or speaking in public, or you're going through a divorce. Think about how you can deal with this scary thing. To keep your mind off flying, you travel with friends; or to help with your speaking, you've hired a coach. If it's divorce, maybe you've begun work with a therapist. All of these kinds of actions show that you're on the right track to living a positive and fear-FULL life, which means you feel the fear yet you know how to brace yourself for the scary thing.

But, fear isn't done yet. Fear loves to show up when you least expect it. Even after you feel like you've gotten a handle on the scary thing, you have to be prepared.

Take, for example, divorce. I have friends who have gone through it and made it to the other side, my husband included. Yet, the pain and guilt of it never quite go away. So you have to train for that race. You have to be mentally prepared for fear hitting you when you least expect it. Fear of going back to court, fear of your kids hating you, fear of not having enough money to pay the bills on your own. It could be six years post-divorce and fear will show up in ways you don't expect and try to force you down a black hole of self-hate. Fear wants you to go back to where you were in the throes of the divorce instead of moving on and believing you are worthy of love.

Fear will continue to follow you, even after you've learned to befriend it. I know this firsthand! I speak for a living and have spent most of my life performing in some capacity. Yet, it's easy to fill with self-doubt right before I take the stage. Public speaking never gets easier, you just get stronger and better. Even after years of speaking, fear still shows up to try and stop me from getting up on that stage and rocking it.

How, you may ask, do you prepare for this never-ending story of fear? You need to tell yourself that you love yourself and then just keep on doing brave things. There are three things I always do before I step onto any stage to help me handle the never-ending "pretalk jitters":

1. I power-pose for two minutes, either backstage or in a bathroom stall, to raise my vibration and step into my power.[20]

2. I put a song in my earbuds that pumps me up and I jam out—usually "Unstoppable" by Sia does the trick.

3. I tell myself I love myself. This simple ritual has now become something my brain expects in order to perform at my best, and I've created a habit that has trained my mind to know that no matter what happens, we will have fun and I will be okay.

It never gets easier, you just get stronger. Find comfort in this journey, and know that you are not alone: we are all scared.

MAKE FEAR YOUR BUSINESS PARTNER

None of us really knows what we are doing. We are all big huge 'fraidy cats who are out there trying new things and hoping we don't fall on our faces. And guess

---

20   https://www.ted.com/talks/amy_cuddy_your_body_language_shapes_who_you_are.

what—that's okay! It's okay to not have it all figured out, to fall down, to fail, to freak out. It's okay to feel afraid. It really is. What's not okay is letting any of this stop you. You can FEEL it, but you can't BE it.

As a business owner who is responsible for making my own money, my never-ending fear story is huge. I could be crushing it financially and doing really brave things in my business, yet I'm constantly afraid in the back of my head that I will run out of money, that no one will hire me, that I'm not a good speaker, or that I'll go out of business and become irrelevant. Because I know this is my never-ending fear story, however, I welcome it to my party. I don't try to shake it. I prepare for it by addressing each fear with action and preparation. As much as fear can be a block in your life, it can also be a gift keeping you hungry, focused, and motivated to stay in forward momentum. It can help you *improve* your business.

Fear can fuel your focus. Fear of running out of money keeps you saving more than you spend. Fear of becoming irrelevant keeps you reading and learning. Fear of getting sick keeps you eating well and working out. Fear can also help you lead with more grace and compassion, once you can see through people's mistakes and speak to the fears that underlie those missteps. Say someone on your team continues to stall on a project or keeps making excuses for why something isn't getting done. Instead of managing the "tactic," why not manage the fear? Why not find out what it is that they are afraid of, then help manage that? You will move from "boss" to mentor, and this is a powerful shift. One that inspires people to level up.

When you shift from avoiding fear to actually wanting it to become a part of your business, you've changed the conversation. You go from worried to warrior! You are ready to address your fears head-on because you realize YOU are the boss, YOU call the shots, and this is YOUR life party. Fear is welcome, yet fear is not allowed to be in charge or take the wheel. Ever. And you know this because you are now a badass Fear Boss.

Go from worried to warrior!

TALK IT OUT

Conversations are a part of life. You have conversations with your friends, your family, your kids, your leadership, and your team. These conversations allow you to check in, stay in touch, and make things happen. Through them, you can get on the same page, handle conflict, and negotiate. It's almost impossible to imagine a day of your life going by without it including talking with someone, having a conversation. Why, then, don't we have conversations with our fears?

When reading *Big Magic* by Elizabeth Gilbert, I was struck by the way she posed this idea of literally talking to our fear. She writes: "I cordially invite fear to come along with me everywhere I go. I even have a welcoming speech prepared for fear, which I deliver right before embarking upon any new project or big adventure."

After reading this, I wrote a welcome speech of my own for my fear:

Dearest Fear,

Hi and thank you so much for being with me today. I have to tell you that you really are incredible at what you do. You always keep me safe and remind me I'm alive. Thank you for that. That said, today I have to give a big speech and it's really important that I do great and deliver value for the audience, so I need you to chill for a minute and grab a seat in the front row so you can watch me crush it. When the speech is done and I'm in the taxi on the way to the airport, you are welcome to come on back to make sure I travel safely. But, for now, I got this. Thank you, love you.

xoxo,
Judith

(PS—I always use my "formal" name when addressing fear so I feel like a real "#FearBoss")

Instead of trying to go to war against your fear, why not try to make space for it? Before the presentation, before the interview, before the confrontation, before the date, take a deep breath and welcome your fear. Thank it, love it, let it stretch out, and then gently remind fear that you are the boss, and it is not. You'll have plenty of opportunities to talk to fear because you do scary things every day.

Each time you simply start noticing when fear shows up in your life, you can create a habit for yourself to start saying hello right away, which shows your fear that you are not only aware of its presence but you are also in control of the outcome, not fear. This shifts the power from fear over to you. This allows you to take a deep breath and move forward. I do this all the time when I feel a panic attack coming on. I literally say to the panic (aka fear), "Oh, hey there, panic. You again? Not today. We are good. I am good. My body is good. I can breathe. Everything is fine over here. You don't need to be here right now."

If I can, I speak this out loud very firmly, and usually my body starts to relax within seconds. You'll be faced with fear of one type or another every day. Some fears are the usual suspects—things that show up all the time—and some are new fears. This approach gives you the gift of getting the chance to try again and get stronger in your ability to manage fear's control over you.

EVERY DAY YOU ARE REBORN

In improv theater, our onstage mistakes and imperfections are seen as gifts. These golden opportunities are where we try something, fail, learn, grow—and then rinse and repeat. An improv teacher of mine used to tell us before every show, "Go out there and fail, fail hard!" This gave us permission to f*ck things up. This lesson was so powerful to me because it was the opposite of what was happening in my corporate environment. At work and in business, I felt like I had to be the best, always. I had to stay in the lines, not ruffle any feathers, and follow the rules. In improv it was the opposite, however; each time I stepped onstage, I had permission to be myself and do what felt right. No matter what happened onstage, even if I hated how I performed, I would wake up the next day with a chance to try again.

This idea of being "reborn" each day can give you the permission slip you need to be okay failing at something or making a mistake, because you know that tomorrow you'll get another chance. You can now take what you've learned from your failure and apply its lessons to your next go—at bat, onstage, in the sales meeting, as a parent, or as a friend. So yes, you are starting again; but you now have knowledge you didn't have before, which can make you a little more courageous. You start doing this enough, and you'll begin to retrain the way your brain processes failures and fear. You go from thinking *I better avoid that* to thinking *I can't wait to see what I learn!* You will start changing that inner dialogue from *What if things go wrong?* to *Yay, a plot twist!*

Each time you fail, you take note of what you learned, pick yourself up, and try again. When you do this, you are working out your bravery muscle. And just like lifting weights at a gym, the more you do it, the stronger you get. It may not get easier, but you WILL get stronger.

The same is true for you as a leader. You will have tough days. You'll mess up, make a bad call, lose an account, or have to fire someone. That night you will go to bed worrying, but when you wake up the next day, you'll have a fresh start. It's like you are born again. It's a brand-new day to make new choices, develop improved habits, and love yourself a little bit more. When you look at each day as an opportunity to start over, you're giving yourself permission to fail. You'll feel more comfortable trying new things, and you'll find it easier to show yourself some grace.

Failure can be a requirement in leveling up because it shapes your life story. Each time you fail, you add powerful lessons into each chapter of your life book. If you think about your life as a book, do you have enough stories, plot twists, new adventures, and lessons learned to fill the chapters? I don't know about you, but I've never met an interesting person with a boring story. You need plot twists, failures, and mistakes to shape your life book into the bestseller it was born to be.

When you start celebrating failure like you celebrate birthdays, you disarm fear and arm action. And in the process, you'll become an incredible example to those around you . . . encouraging them to fail forward. Before you know it, YOU are the one writing "permission to fail" slips for those around you and then celebrating each time they add a new chapter into their own life book.

The Victory Lap

You do so much every day for your family, your friends, at work, and especially as you are out there being a Fear Boss. When was the last time you took a moment to look around at all you have accomplished? Fear can keep us so busy rushing toward this imaginary finish line in our head that we forget to just stop for a minute and acknowledge how far we've come in the first place.

Just the other day I was on the phone with a friend who said, "Judi, I know you have a million things going on, yet have you stopped for a second to just think about and celebrate all you've accomplished the past six months?" That question stopped me in my tracks, because no, I hadn't. I'm so focused on each task in my life and I get obsessed with goals I've set for myself that I've forgotten to look around and take it all in.

You deserve a victory lap. And fear hates victory laps because when you stop, pause, and reflect on all the brave things you do every day, you'll fill your soul up with encouragement and an internal self-pride that can be hard to stop.

According to Wikipedia, a victory lap is when a race car driver takes an extra lap of the racetrack after winning a race. This lap, driven at a pretty slow pace, allows the driver to celebrate their victory and gives the audience an opportunity to congratulate and honor everybody who competed. Any *Talladega Nights* fan out there knows "Ricky Bobby" loved taking his victory laps! Think about how you might channel your inner Ricky Bobby and take more victory laps from time to time. You are winning races in your life all the time. Raising good kids, staying healthy, crushing it at work. You deserve to celebrate your success. You deserve to celebrate when you've bossed up to a fear. Doing this helps you not only disarm fear, but also look forward to doing more brave things because you know the victory lap is imminent. Perhaps you reward yourself with a massage, a bubble bath, brunch with friends, new jeans, or a day trip somewhere fun. Whatever you choose, putting time aside to take a victory lap is a powerful way to recognize the courage it takes every day to do all that you do.

Alex Toussaint always makes us take a victory lap the last few minutes of the ride in our Peloton classes. He challenges us to take a few minutes, sometimes longer, to soak up all the good we just did for our bodies. We high-five our classmates and ourselves. This got me wondering: Why do I do this on my bike and not any other time? It's important for us to celebrate our health, our lives, our stories, and all the little things that have to happen every day for us to keep moving forward.

You are out there doing badass things, and most people don't get to see them. All the little pieces of your life puzzle are moving strategically into place; while this may look effortless, you know that on the other side of that puzzle is a Fear BOSS who is working their ass off. You deserve to celebrate yourself. You deserve a moment to step back and observe all you've done and created and started. So take that victory lap—hell, take two of them!

IT'S OKAY TO BE THE HERO OF YOUR OWN STORY

You don't need anyone else to come save you. You don't need an amazing mom or supportive dad. You don't need any external thing or material possession to be your hero. No amount of money, sex, drugs, success, or Louis Vuitton bags will fill the void of regret. Only YOU can fill that void with self-love and being a Fear Boss. While heroes are great, and I certainly have a few, the reality is that I know I'm the real hero in my life story, and so are YOU in yours. Every time you push yourself outside your comfort zone and do things you never knew you were capable of, you are crushing comfort zones and slaying doubt.

A real hero trains for the race all summer and finishes the marathon with heart-pumping pride. A real hero is an exhausted mother of two who goes back to work despite her self-doubt. A real hero skips happy hour to hit the gym, losing fifty pounds along the way. A real hero doesn't give away her body to find love, because she knows she's a gift. A real hero saves for a year to renovate her dream house and fills with pride each time she writes a check. All of the things, big or small, that you accomplish on the regular make up your life story—and they are all YOU! Not anyone or anything else. The second you realize that YOU are the real hero in your life story, you step into your power and tighten up your courage cape.

YOU are all you need to save yourself from a life of mediocrity. You are all you need to choose courage over comfort. You must step up if you want to design the life of your dreams. When fear is your homeboy, you actively seek out opportunities to level up, even when you are afraid, because deep down nothing is scarier than mediocrity and living with regret. Every day, you are either making choices to move further away from your goals or you are making boss moves to get closer to them.

Choose to be your own hero and help yourself reach these goals by taking action every single day. This takes the courage to trust yourself enough to know that you must go scared, knowing that fear will keep you safe and that you won't allow fear to keep you stuck.

THE BEST BET YOU'LL EVER MAKE

Every day you place bets. Now, you may be thinking . . . no way . . . not me . . . I'm not a gambling kind of person. But you are. You gamble with your time, your heart, your money, your career, your friends, your family—all with zero guarantees. Thirty years from now, your partner could up and leave you. You could spend decades working for a company and they could just lay you off, with no explanation. You could save for retirement all your life only to watch the stock market crash. All of this could happen. This possibility should not scare you, however; this is a "fear is my homeboy" moment. It should help you take action and infuse courage into your bones.

Jobs, love, and money will come and go, but *you* will always be a constant in your life, regardless of how bad the situation is. This is why it's so important to love yo'self first and know that you hold all the power. You can either let your past, or your fear of how your story could unfold, keep you stuck—or you can let your past, and your actions in the present, fuel your future.

When you bet on you, not anything or anyone else, you start to live with a confidence that allows you to handle all the stuff (self-doubt, anxiety, guilt, shame) fear will throw at you, and to handle it like a real boss. This means you are betting your success, your physical health, your mental health, your career, your happiness, and your financial security on yourself. You aren't waiting for anything or anyone else to help you get it. You are taking action every day to make sure you have your own back. Most of us will have love and support in our lives, and most of us get help along the way, which is such an amazing privilege. Yet you must realize that all of it could be gone tomorrow. What are you doing today to prepare yourself should the unexpected happen?

I ended up moving to Chicago because I had been dumped. Yep, crying on the bathroom floor, snot dripping out of my nose, rock-bottom dumped. Six months earlier, I'd moved from St. Louis to a crappy small town for love, full of hope and excitement. Then, he dumped my ass. I was heartbroken, embarrassed, pissed off, and angry. But I chose to bet on myself, not on him. Instead of running back home to St. Louis where things were safe, I got a new job, rented a U-Haul, packed all my stuff, and drove to Chicago to start fresh. At the time, I knew only three people, had never lived anywhere new by myself, and was scared to death.

This moment of betting on myself, trusting myself, and loving myself got me up off that bathroom floor and put into motion a chain of events that led to the rest of my life. The simple act of renting the U-Haul and putting the keys in the ignition to begin the drive to Chicago kicked in the magic of momentum and started a chain reaction of new opportunities—because now I was in the driver's seat. Quite literally. *(I drove that massive U-Haul all by myself!)* I knew that only I had the power to write a new story, and it was up to me to be the hero of my own story. I could sit around and cry about it, or I could get my sh*t together and do something about it. Taking action even when you aren't sure how it's going to work out is what happens when you bet on yourself instead of on fear. When you bet on fear, you are playing it safe, because safe feels good. When you bet on yourself, you leap into the unknown because you trust yourself more than anyone or anything else. When you do this, your universe can only do one thing: expand! Fear cannot stand with faith. Period.

Contrary to what you may think or believe about yourself, you are a betting Fear Boss and you bet on yourself every day. This is the best kind of bet because it walks bliss right into your front door.

Follow Your Bliss

When you're about forty years old, it really hits you how short life is. Your parents start getting older, you lose people you love or see people your age get sick, you watch your old college friends' kids become college kids themselves, and you quickly wonder where the past twenty years went. It starts to feel like things are moving at the speed of light. Spoiler alert: things ARE moving at the speed of light! You don't have to wait until you're fortysomething to realize this, and no matter what age you are, it's never too late to take action *now* on what it is that you *really* want. You don't have to go through the motions any longer! Let's see what this might look like.

Your alarm goes off at 6:00 a.m. You hit snooze a few times, then finally get up. You go through your regular routine. Wash face, shower, take vitamins, make coffee, get dressed, drive to work. You like your job, but you aren't lit up like you thought you'd be at this age. But you brush it off, settle in at your desk, and because you mentally can't bring yourself to begin the day, you scroll through social media to kill some time. Your feed shows you that some of your friends are on vacation in Italy, a cousin is getting married in Ireland, and a coworker just bought a new lake house. You think, *Ugh, I can't remember the last time I even took a vacation*, and instantly feel sad and jealous. When you get back to work, you open your email to an angry client who copied your boss. You then have a mild panic attack and think, *This cannot be my life for the next thirty years.*

Fear Boss, you don't have to suffer. There is a better way! Following your bliss doesn't mean that every day is full of magical unicorns and rainbows, but it does mean that you choose to do the hard work required in order to get the life you deserve. This requires you to get uncomfortable and start taking action so you can figure out what bliss might look like for you. Maybe it starts by simply booking a vacation to reflect and rest. Maybe you begin networking to find a new job. Maybe you take a class or start reading more books to get inspired. You don't have to be miserable. Misery is a side effect of a fear-based life. Success is a side effect of courage.

Misery is a side effect of a fear-based life. Success is a side effect of courage.

Why in the hell do you keep waiting for someday to be happy when you deserve to be happy right now? Someday I'll have more time. Someday I'll have my dream job. Someday I'll have more money. Someday I'll have more connections. You will be waiting for someday your whole life. We need to find our bliss now. Bliss is the process of peeling away the darkness to shed light on who it is that you really are. It's where happiness, fulfillment, and truth intersect. This means you do things that make you happy, you do work that leaves you feeling fulfilled, and you live in a way that's authentic to who you really are. When all three of these things are in motion, happiness, fulfillment, and truth, you are following your bliss!

In order to *find your bliss,* you have to have the courage to shake things up and snap yourself out of "poor me " mode and into "why the hell not me" mode! When Fear Is Your Homeboy, you know that in order to find your bliss, you have to have the courage to stop from time to time in order to check in with yourself. Are you going through the motions? Have you become complacent? Are you on autopilot? If you don't like your answers to these questions, you have to put a plan in place so you can start taking action toward the life you really want. You deserve to be happy. You can be fulfilled. You are allowed to live your truth.

Happiness is universal. We all want to feel happy. We surround ourselves with people we love, we go on vacation, we eat the dessert—we do all these things to bring more happiness into our lives. We also seek fulfillment, wanting to feel a deep connection to what we do. Fulfillment helps us get out of bed in the morning and feel proud of the work we do. Truth is being exactly who you are and not apologizing for it. There is nothing fear hates more than watching you courageously being exactly, and authentically, who you were born to be.

While the components of bliss will be shared by lots of us, the actual appearance of bliss is going to look different in each of our lives. Right now, for me, bliss is eating a warm chocolate-chip cookie right out of the oven (happiness); it's being my own boss; it's helping people do brave things by speaking onstage (fulfillment); it's putting stickers all over my suitcase because I can; it's infusing my love of hip-hop into the things I create (my truth). Think about what your happiness, fulfillment, and truth are and how they show up in your life. Are they combining into bliss?

You are allowed to love your life. You are allowed to love what you do and who you do it with. Bliss is your right, not a privilege reserved for the lucky few who just so happen to "have it all." When you crack the bliss code, you'll find a way to fend off fear, because fear doesn't know what to do with the power of bliss. You'll also inspire everyone around you! Start a badass bliss chain reaction.

Bliss is your right, not a privilege reserved for the lucky few who just so happen to "have it all."

In Conclusion

Fear is always the strongest at the finish line. Fear never wants you to finish the race because the second you finish, fear has nowhere to go. So, here you are . . . about to finish reading this book, which means you have a new perspective on your fear and new tools to deal with it. And fear is not happy about that . . . fear is actually kind of pissed off because you are stronger now than when you started reading this book. And with that comes power.

When you make fear your homeboy, you are a warrior, not a worrier. It means you are ready to write a new story and flip the script on fear. It means you are ready to take your power back. It means you love yo'self, you trust yourself, you are ready to boss up, you have a tribe that supports you, and you realize action is your secret weapon.

The bottom line is this: no one is coming to save you. It's up to you to make things happen. You must be the hero of your own story. Every single day, fear is trying to stop that from happening because fear loves the limelight and wants to be the hero of your story. Every day, fear wants to steal your joy and rob you of opportunities to earn more, be more, and do more. Every single day. Fear is a relentless little devil and is determined as hell. Fear will never give up, so trying to outrun it or get rid of it is the wrong approach.

The way in, through, and around your fear is to make space for it. Show up to it. And Make Fear Your Homeboy!

How to Make Fear Your Homeboy
AND BE A FEARFULLY COURAGEOUS #FEARBOSS:

1. Write a "Dear Fear" letter.

Write a letter to your fear! Make it clear what you will, and will not, allow. You can have different letters for different fears. For example, you can have a "dear fear" letter for before you have to speak in public and also a "dear fear" letter for before any scary doctor's appointment. Anytime you encounter this scary thing, write your letter and read it aloud. Then keep it somewhere you can easily access it to remind yourself that you are in control, not fear.

2. Keep a failure journal.

As you go out there and do brave things, you will make mistakes and fail from time to time. Good! This means you are beta testing new things and adding chapters to your life story. Remember: no mistakes, only gifts! So make sure you take the time to write down the stories, lessons, and ideas you learned from each mistake or failure along the way. You never know how the stories and lessons can come back to help you, or someone else, later. Use an actual notebook, create one in Evernote, or build a spreadsheet in Google Sheets. Write the "failure" at the top and then have three columns: 1. What went right?; 2. What I learned?; 3. What stories can I tell? Notice that these questions force you to focus on the positive outcomes and kick the negative ones to the curb.

3. Rehearse your bliss.

Each morning before you start your day, or touch your phone, rehearse who you will be that day. What is the ideal state of being you desire to be in today? Then literally dress rehearse how you want the day to go, who you want to be, how you want to act, what choices you'll make, and how you'll be brave. If you have a big presentation today, you will literally see yourself crushing it. If you have to have a tough conversation, you watch yourself handling the confrontation with ease. This is best done in bed before you get up for the day, or in the shower as the water is waking you up. Any private moment or space works.

4. Plan your victory laps.

Start noticing all the brave things you do every day. And start rewarding yourself each time you accomplish things when the odds are stacked against you. You set up the blog—reward yourself with a massage! You put your name in the hat for the promotion—book a mani-pedi. You had the kids to yourself all week with no extra help—take a hot *(uninterrupted!)* bubble bath with a juicy magazine for a whole hour. You worked out four days this week—treat yo'self to a new pair of cute yoga pants!

5. Start a #FearIsMyHomeboy movement.

Begin this within your own circle, personally and professionally, and become a fear hero for someone else.

- Share this, and other personal development books, with your team and people you love.

- Start a #FearBoss circle with your friends or colleagues at work as a way to discuss how you can bring more happiness into your life every day, seek out opportunities to be more brave, and take action to boss up on your bliss.

- Decide to put something in motion right now and use this Fear Is My Homeboy card to make it official. Write a goal, dream, or desire that you will move forward now that Fear Is Your Homeboy. Take a photo and share it on social using #FearIsMyHomeboy so I can cheer you on and/or post it somewhere visible in your office, or at home, so you are always reminded what a #FearBoss you are.

Shameless Plug

If you've made it to the end of this book, YOU ARE A BADASS #FearBOSS!!! Cue the confetti, cue the balloons, cue the high fives and bear hugs. Thank you for investing your time here. It's been my honor to create it for you. I hope you had as much fun reading it as I did creating it.

If you are screaming *Hell YES* and craving more . . . there are a few ways to stay connected and work with me:

1. You can learn more about the work I do by visiting my website at www. judiholler.com.

2. You can hire me to speak at your next meeting or convention. I offer keynote speeches and workshops all designed using the experimental principles of improv theater to help you navigate the unscripted stage of everyday life so you (and your team!) can transform fear into your secret weapon, slay doubt, and succeed the way YOU want to succeed! I love working with women, sales teams, emerging leaders and students, creatives, and entrepreneurs. You can reach me at hello@judiholler.com.

3. You can sign up for my newsletter, "The Friday #FearBoss Five," right on the homepage of my website at www.judiholler.com. This newsletter is a party in your inbox every Friday and shares weekly resources, tools, ideas, and inspiration that will empower you to smash those comfort zones. This is also the best place to stay in touch with #AllTheThings, and my newsletter list is always the first to know when we launch a new product,

create a program, conduct a live event, or release anything new in the Fear Boss Community.

4. You can keep the fear party going by tuning into *The #FearBoss Show* podcast on your favorite podcast platform. The mission of the podcast is to EMPOWER you to live a braver life, lead braver teams, and smash comfort zones.

5. Join the Fear Boss community on Facebook! If you want to connect with like-minded Fear Bosses all over the world who are out there smashing comfort zones and making the world a braver place, our Facebook group is the perfect place to get inspired. The #FearBoss Fam group page is on Facebook at

   https://facebook.com/groups/fearboss

6. You can follow me on social media and keep the fear party going! I am always sharing tools, resources, and ideas to help you slay doubt and manage fear.

   @JudiHoller

   https://facebook.com/FearIsMyHomeboy

   https://www.youtube.com/c/JudiHoller

   @JudiHoller

Acknowledgments

"Say yes, and you'll figure it out afterwards."

—TINA FEY

Saying yes to writing this book was one of the scariest, most amazing, challenging, and fun things I've ever done professionally. I could not have made it happen without the badass tribe of incredible people who have been in my corner since day one. Let's get this gratitude party started, shall we?!

First, there wouldn't be a book without my publisher, Greenleaf Book Group! A huge thank-you to the entire team at Greenleaf for believing in me, for loving Fear Is My Homeboy® as much as I do, and for saying YES to the idea! I especially want to thank the incredible AprilJo Murphy for helping me organize all my words and ideas into a beautifully written book and for teaching me so much about writing! To Rachael for designing such a beautiful cover and interior that exceeded ALL expectations, and to each editor who gave their time to diligently review every page and each word with such love, focus, and brain power. I'm in awe of your talent.

To Scott, my husband and my best friend, I cannot thank you enough for your countless hours of advice and steady counsel, for listening to me talk waaaaaay too much about work (and this book!), and for cheering me on every step of the way as I build my business and chase my dreams. While life isn't easy, we get stronger together and my favorite part, we have so much damn fun doing it! Thank you, my love. For all of it. #ArrowForward

To my family, and all my friends who are family, you know who you are! I'd be lost without you, and I'm so proud to have each one of you in my life. Thank you for all the love, support, champagne, and high fives as this book came to life. I love love love you all!

To my #EventProf, #EventBOSS, and meeting industry family and friends. When I quit my job to start my company full-time, you came in HOT, being the first to hire me, and you keep doing so. I'm so grateful; it's hard to find the words. I am proud to be a meeting professional and even more proud to be trusted with your members, your teams, and your organizations when hired to keynote and/or emcee your events. Meetings do mean business; and when we meet, we change the world!

To every improv teacher at the Second City Training Center Conservatory whom I had the honor of learning from. You changed my damn life. Look, those line-filled notebooks I had in every class (nerd alert!) got put to good use after all! And to all my fellow improvisers and castmates that I've played, and created, with over the years. We've done shows in basements, bars, deli shops, at midnight, with two people watching, with two hundred—it never mattered; we are always failing forward. Even when we visited that damn hat shop. Your talent, badassery, energy, and brilliance helped me keep showing up . . . especially when things got scary.

To Heather Allison Smith—I'm so glad you attended that MPI STL lunch back in 2003. Thank you for hiring me and giving me my first job in the meetings business with zero experience. It was a boomerang I caught and have never let go of. And Holly, thank you for making me attend!

To my business coach, Jane Atkinson. Your advice and support as I grow my business has been the steady counsel I need when I don't know what to do next, when I get way too in my head, and especially when I feel afraid. Thank you for listening, guiding, pushing, and cheering me on.

To all the incredible authors and thought leaders mentioned in this book, I stand on the shoulders of giants!! The books on my shelves have become some of my best friends. Because you had the courage to share your ideas, you've not only changed the world, you most certainly have changed mine. Thank you for being a part of this book, and I hope those reading this book love you as much as I do.

To everyone on the HOLLA Team who has helped me build my dream job and bring my ideas to life—YOU are changing the world with me! Amanda, my ninja and right-hand HOLLA woman, I can't even! I'm so glad our worlds collided. Thank you for believing in me, trusting me, and helping me keep my shit together—you are a goddess. To Peter and Cait at Front Edge Digital, from the beginning you believed, and I cannot thank you enough for all the ways you continue to support me and my growing business. To every creative I've hired in any capacity to help me grow my business over the past two years with dope video edits, photography, marketing, and accounting support . . . THANK YOU for your talent, time, and rock-star skills!

To "The Friday FAB Five Tribe." You guys have been with me from the beginning and I love you! I can't thank you enough for being a part of my life, for supporting my work, this book, and most of all for inspiring me more than you can even imagine. The email, posts, DMs, and notes I receive from you about all the brave things you do every day are my FUEL, and it's humbling to watch so many of you step into your power as a true #FearBoss. I'm so damn proud of you all, and thank you for all your support. (And yes, don't worry, there will be an email on Friday!!)

And finally, to you, the reader. Thank you for spending money on this book, for spending your time reading it, and for sharing it with other fear bosses you love. I'm so glad you are here!

About the Author

JUDI HOLLER owns a creative company that is on a mission to empower people to live braver lives and help leaders lead braver teams. Her work takes the experimental principles of the improv theatre and helps you apply them to the unscripted stage of everyday life. These ideas will teach you that while you'll never be "fearless" you can get really good at FEARING FEAR LESS! Judi is a professionally trained improviser and alumna of the Second City Training Center Conservatory in Chicago, Illinois. Judi started working in the hospitality industry at the age of thirteen and has spent the past fifteen years working in the convention and meetings industry, specializing in sales and marketing for companies like Marriott, Omni, and Starwood Hotels before starting her company, HOLLA! Productions, in 2013.

Judi was born and raised in St. Louis, Missouri, and spent ten years living in Chicago, studying improv by night and growing her career by day. Judi now resides in Hudson, Ohio, with her husband, Scott, and their amazingly adorable golden retriever, Tito. Judi is a proud stepmom to three badass boys—Sean, Sam, and Jack. She is also a gushing godmother and auntie to niece, Kiley Grace, and nephews, Finnegan and Jaxson.

When Judi is not keynoting conferences, working as a corporate event emcee/moderator, writing, and creating cool stuff for you, she is most likely on her Peloton bike, deep in a book, or testing out a new fear experiment.

Judi likes her books non-digital, her wine bubbly, and her music hip-hop.